First World War
and Army of Occupation
War Diary
France, Belgium and Germany

21 DIVISION
Divisional Troops
94 Brigade Royal Field Artillery
7 September 1915 - 30 April 1919

WO95/2141/3

The Naval & Military Press Ltd
www.nmarchive.com
Published in association with The National Archives

Published by

The Naval & Military Press Ltd

Unit 10 Ridgewood Industrial Park,

Uckfield, East Sussex,

TN22 5QE England

Tel: +44 (0) 1825 749494

www.naval-military-press.com

www.nmarchive.com

This diary has been reprinted in facsimile from the original. Any imperfections are inevitably reproduced and the quality may fall short of modern type and cartographic standards.

© **Crown Copyright**
Images reproduced by permission of The National Archives, London, England, 2015.

Contents

Document type	Place/Title	Date From	Date To
Heading	WO95/2141/3 21 Division 94th Bde R.F.A. Sept 1915-Apl 1919		
Heading	21st Division 94th Bde R.F.A. Sep 1915-Apr 1919		
Heading	War Diary Headquarters, 94th Brigade, R.F.A. (21st Division) September (7.9.15 To 30.9.15) 1915 Apr 19		
War Diary	Astron Clenton	07/09/1915	30/09/1915
Heading	21st Division 94th Bde. R.F.A. Vol 2 Oct 15		
War Diary		01/10/1915	30/10/1915
Heading	21st Division 94th Bde. R.F.A. Vol 3 Nov 15		
War Diary	Armentieres	01/11/1915	30/11/1915
Heading	21st Divisional Artillery. 94th Brigade R.F.A. January 1916		
War Diary	Armentieres	01/01/1916	11/01/1916
War Diary	Armentieres	05/12/1915	30/12/1915
War Diary		11/01/1916	30/01/1916
Heading	21st Divisional Artillery 94th Brigade R.F.A. February 1916		
War Diary	Armentieres	11/02/1916	28/02/1916
Heading	21st Divisional Artillery 94th Brigade R.F.A. March 1916		
War Diary	Armentieres	05/03/1916	23/03/1916
War Diary	Caestre	23/03/1916	31/03/1916
Heading	21st Divisional Artillery. 94th Brigade R.F.A. April 1916		
War Diary	Daours Albert	01/04/1916	30/04/1916
Heading	21st Divisional Artillery 94th Brigade R.F.A. May 1916		
War Diary	Meaulte (Albert)	30/04/1916	10/05/1916
War Diary	Meaulte	14/05/1916	29/05/1916
Miscellaneous	To D.A.G 3rd Echelon	03/06/1916	03/06/1916
Heading	21st Divisional Artillery 94th Brigade R.F.A. June 1916		
War Diary	Meaulte	27/05/1916	30/06/1916
War Diary	Gegette	03/06/1916	03/06/1916
Miscellaneous	21st DA War Diary	01/08/1916	01/08/1916
Heading	21st Divisional Artillery 94th Brigade R.F.A. July 1916		
War Diary	Becordel	01/07/1916	30/07/1916
Heading	21st Divisional Artillery 94th Brigade R.F.A. August 1916		
War Diary		31/07/1916	24/08/1916
Heading	21st Divisional Artillery. 94th Brigade R.F.A. September 1916		
War Diary	Arras	03/09/1916	15/09/1916
War Diary	Bntauban	15/09/1916	30/09/1916
War Diary		14/09/1916	30/09/1916
Heading	21st Divisional Artillery. 94th Brigade R.F.A. October 1916		
War Diary	Somme	01/10/1916	22/10/1916
War Diary	Field	01/10/1916	14/10/1916
Heading	21st Divisional Artillery. 94th Brigade R.F.A. November 1916		
War Diary	Noyelles	06/11/1916	27/11/1916

War Diary		06/11/1916	27/11/1916
War Diary		10/11/1916	25/11/1916
Miscellaneous	21st DA War Diary	26/11/1916	26/11/1916
Heading	21st Divisional Artillery. 94th Brigade R.F.A. December 1916		
War Diary	Quarries Sector	11/12/1916	26/12/1916
War Diary		07/12/1916	24/12/1916
War Diary		03/12/1916	03/12/1916
Heading	21st Div 94th Bde R.F.A. Vol. 4		
War Diary	Noyelles	03/01/1917	04/01/1917
War Diary	Raimbert	15/01/1917	31/01/1917
War Diary		07/01/1917	07/01/1917
War Diary		01/02/1917	22/02/1917
War Diary	Vermelles	04/03/1917	27/03/1917
War Diary	Boiry St. Rictrude	02/04/1917	30/04/1917
War Diary		25/03/1917	30/04/1917
War Diary		27/05/1917	31/05/1917
War Diary	Boiry	02/05/1917	02/05/1917
War Diary	Becquelle	03/05/1917	29/05/1917
War Diary	H.Q T20 d 7.4 St Leger	01/06/1917	16/06/1917
War Diary	H.Q. T20 d 7.4 Sheet 51 SW	02/07/1917	26/07/1917
War Diary		16/07/1917	17/07/1917
War Diary	H. Qrs Trod Sheet 51b SW	01/08/1917	30/09/1917
War Diary		26/09/1917	26/09/1917
War Diary		24/09/1917	24/09/1917
War Diary		12/09/1917	30/09/1917
War Diary		25/09/1917	30/09/1917
War Diary	Dormy House I23a 5.5	01/10/1917	09/10/1917
War Diary	Dormy House	10/10/1917	31/10/1917
War Diary	In The Field	06/10/1917	29/10/1917
War Diary	In The Field	02/10/1917	30/10/1917
War Diary	In The Field	01/10/1917	31/10/1917
War Diary	In The Field	04/10/1917	31/10/1917
War Diary	Holers Dormy House	01/11/1917	15/11/1917
War Diary	Morbecque	17/11/1917	30/11/1917
War Diary	In The Field	01/11/1917	02/12/1917
War Diary	Bde Hd qrs Ste Emilie E 24 L 3.7	03/12/1917	27/12/1917
War Diary	Field	10/12/1917	28/12/1917
War Diary	Field	11/12/1917	11/12/1917
War Diary	H.Q St Emilie E.24 F.3.7 62C. NE	01/01/1918	29/01/1918
War Diary	Field	06/01/1918	06/01/1918
War Diary	H.Q St Emilie E.24 B. 3.7 62C. N.E	01/02/1918	11/02/1918
War Diary	Driencourt	12/02/1918	28/02/1918
War Diary	Field	28/01/1918	28/01/1918
War Diary	Field	19/02/1918	19/02/1918
Heading	21st Div. War Diary Headquarters, 94th Brigade, R.F.A. March (13/30.3.18) 1918		
War Diary	HQ Ste Emilie	13/03/1918	21/03/1918
War Diary	HQ Saulcourt-Longavesnes Road	22/03/1918	22/03/1918
War Diary	HQ Bussu	23/03/1918	24/03/1918
War Diary	HQ Maricourt	24/03/1918	24/03/1918
Miscellaneous	94th Bde. R.F.A.	25/10/1918	25/10/1918
War Diary		25/03/1918	30/03/1918
War Diary		21/03/1918	29/03/1918
War Diary		21/03/1918	28/03/1918

Heading	21st Divisional Artillery. 94th Brigade R.F.A. April 1918			
War Diary	Beaucourt		01/04/1918	11/04/1918
War Diary	H.Q. as Q.33 F 5.5		13/04/1918	14/04/1918
War Diary	H.Q At R.18.c.6.4		19/04/1918	19/04/1918
War Diary	H.Q At R 20 C		23/04/1918	23/04/1918
War Diary	Field		01/04/1918	25/04/1918
War Diary			16/04/1918	29/04/1918
War Diary			26/04/1918	26/04/1918
War Diary	Berthen District		01/05/1918	31/05/1918
War Diary			06/05/1918	21/05/1918
War Diary	France		27/05/1918	27/05/1918
War Diary			05/05/1918	29/05/1918
War Diary			03/06/1918	30/06/1918
War Diary			10/06/1918	10/06/1918
War Diary			05/06/1918	05/06/1918
War Diary			01/06/1918	01/06/1918
War Diary			05/06/1918	05/06/1918
War Diary			01/06/1918	09/06/1918
War Diary			06/06/1918	06/06/1918
War Diary			03/06/1918	09/06/1918
War Diary			01/07/1918	27/07/1918
War Diary	H.Q P.24.d 4.4 (Sh.57)		27/07/1918	30/07/1918
War Diary	H.Q. P.24d.3.5		01/08/1918	24/08/1918
War Diary	H.Q. R.10.b.2.8		25/08/1918	25/08/1918
War Diary	H.Q. M.8.d.8.6		26/08/1918	26/08/1918
War Diary	H.Q. M.17 F. 41		28/08/1918	28/08/1918
War Diary	H.Q N.13.d		31/08/1918	31/08/1918
War Diary	Field		02/08/1918	27/08/1918
War Diary	H.Q. Luisenhof Farm		01/09/1918	03/09/1918
War Diary	H.Q. Surken Rd. N.24.a		03/09/1918	03/09/1918
War Diary	H.Q. Gun Pits O.28 F.1.8		04/09/1918	05/09/1918
War Diary	H.Q Site Of Chateua Sailly Saillsel		05/09/1918	05/09/1918
War Diary	H.Q. Gun Pits V.14.a		06/09/1918	06/09/1918
War Diary	H.Q. V.17.d. 8.5		07/09/1918	30/09/1918
War Diary			04/09/1918	24/09/1918
Heading	War Diary Of 94th Brigade R.F.A. From 1st October 1918 To 31st October 1918 Vol 38			
War Diary	H.Q. On Peziere Villers Guislan Rd		01/10/1918	06/10/1918
War Diary	H.Q. M.22.b. 7.1		06/10/1918	06/10/1918
War Diary	H.Q. S.4.a.8.5		07/10/1918	08/10/1918
War Diary	H.Q. Montecouvey Farm		08/10/1918	10/10/1918
War Diary	H.Q. Inchy		11/10/1918	21/10/1918
War Diary	H.Q. Neuvilly		23/10/1918	23/10/1918
War Diary	H.Q. Ovillers		24/10/1918	26/10/1918
War Diary	H.Q. Vendegies		26/10/1918	31/10/1918
War Diary	A Bty			
War Diary	B Bty			
Heading	War Diary Of 94th Brigade R.F.A. From 1st November 1918 To 30th November 1918			
War Diary	H.Q. Vendegies		01/11/1918	03/11/1918
War Diary	H.Q. Poix-Du-Nord		04/11/1918	07/11/1918
War Diary	H.Q. La Grand Carriere		08/11/1918	15/11/1918
War Diary	H.Q. Neuvilly		16/11/1918	28/11/1918
Heading	War Diary Of 94th Brigade R.F.A. From:- December 1st To December 31st 1918			

War Diary	Neuvilly	01/12/1918	31/12/1918
War Diary	La Chaussee	01/01/1919	31/01/1919
Heading	War Diary Of 94th Brigade R.F.A. From 1st February 1919 To 28th February 1919		
War Diary	La Chaussee	01/02/1919	31/02/1919
War Diary	La Chaussee	01/03/1919	31/03/1919
Heading	War Diary February 1919		
War Diary	La Chaussee	01/04/1919	30/04/1919

21 DIVISION

94th BDE R.F.A
Sept 1915 - Feb. 1919

WO95/2141/3

21ST DIVISION

94TH BDE R.F.A.
SEP 1915-APR 1919

Brigade disembarked
Havre from England
9.9.15.

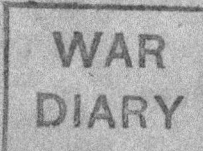

Headquarters,

94th BRIGADE, R.F.A.

(21st Division)

S E P T E M B E R

(7.9.15 to 30.9.15)

1 9 1 5

INTELLIGENCE SUMMARY

Instructions regarding War Diaries and Intelligence Summaries are contained in F.S. Regs., Part II. and the Staff Manual respectively. Title pages will be prepared in manuscript.

(Erase heading not required.)

Place	Date 1915	Hour	Summary of Events and Information	Remarks and references to Appendices
Audru Chatam	Sept 7		B, C & D Batteries entrained	
	8		"A" Bty and Column 1st H.A. Bde entrained – All arrived Southampton and entrained for HAVRE	
	9		All marched R.D. B – A Batteries and H.Q. Brs entrained for AUDRICQUE	
	10		Amm (Column) C & D Batteries entrained for AUDRICQUE – All detrained and marched to RUMINGHEM and billeted (infantile – Supply, hay, both rations r/forage)	
	14		Marched to STAPLE billeted – Supply, late and short.	
	15		Marched to METEREN billeted	
	17		B Officers to trenches for instruction	
	18		O.C. went to trenches and returned	
	19		Officers returned	
	21		Marched to GUARBECQUE billeted	
	22		Marched to BUSNETTE billeted	
	23		Marched 10.30 p.m.	
	25		Arrived HALINCOURT 5 a.m. bivouac til 11 a.m. then marched to MAZINGARBE. O.C. and Adjutant went to join H. Qr. 62nd Inf. Bde who marched off about 2 pm. Batteries & Amm Column arrived 5.30 pm bivouaced. O.C. ordered to report to H.Q. Box 63rd Inf. Bde (east of track of LOOS Road) – met Brig Gen NIKALLS 11 p.m. told to attend	

(1)

INTELLIGENCE SUMMARY.

(Erase heading not required.)

Place	Date 1915	Hour	Summary of Events and Information	Remarks and references to Appendices
	Sept/25		Officers to reconnoitre for positions and line of advance - Capt Corry and Capt Franklyn visit. B.C.'s report at 21st D.A. 2.30 am 26th. Lees horse all confusion and difficult to move either way. Infantry going into trenches on N. of road.	
	" 26		145 am Corry and Franklyn returned and reported - O.O. to 21st D.A. 2.30 am - Brit.s Bombardmentis after R.A. orders made out, sent word to Batteries to move off 9 am, after meeting of D.A. at Le ROUTOIRE at 8 am - Batteries advanced along Loos road. O.C. Brit to advance for one Battery, O.C. finded on hry'm[?] crest which was under heavy fire and met hy'jd Gnrls 680 who showed a "keep" on map. An advance arranged and Batteries sent for. When advance stopped by heavy shelling of crest of hill, no advance of infantry at Kruchoy's on were forced to find. No Batteries registered on their allotted targets - D Battery and E Battery on an advance of Gnrsns N.W. of BOIS HUGO and E Battery on to Lament in spurs of Hill 70. All Batteries fire was ordered to remain at 11 am for the infantry attack to advance and open out 11·5 at target range. The infantry however was pulling back at 10·45 am. Shelling fire opened on the Batteries from N and S - HE and Shrapnel	

INTELLIGENCE SUMMARY

(Erase heading not required.)

Place	Date	Hour	Summary of Events and Information	Remarks and references to Appendices
	Sept 26		Major Watson and F Hill with Infantry were finding tuck and the Brigade was to relieve – hurried up Major Kenny then gun teams – Mobiled under heavy fire but soon men and horses in entrenchment and retirement which was followed. Came into action again (B.22.c) but did not fire – Ammunition 3 killed 10 wounded 4 gunners, horses 11. Bryce and Thompson – Many Infantry passing through the position were stories and fed and returned to trenches. Expended 438 rounds.	Sept 36 c NW J/100000
	27		Reported at 6 am at DAHQ – received orders to stay in present position and register the targets allotted, finished by 1 pm – Received report that Lieut Aitchison was wounded in front trench – to evacuate him from modern Sponbone – 2nd Lieut Stuart who was 3.0.0. was wounded in right arm. Expended 551 rounds	
	28		Many gun shells fell near wagon line, gun drifted through them & removed casualties from it	
	29		Early morning shells came near in morning – Artillery fire from 3.45 pm to 5.30 pm HE shell fire was heavy in Brigade BOIS HUGO – from 3.45 pm to DA was in Exchange position of A+D batteries, woke up at 6 pm reported to DA. New BdC batteries N.S. of Loos Road near MAROC Village. Bye gunner home and withdrew and advancing fire at 9.15 pm Ammunition Batteries home and B.96th Bde Arty. and contacted A and D Batteries position.	

INTELLIGENCE SUMMARY.

(Erase heading not required.)

Place	Date 1915	Hour	Summary of Events and Information	Remarks and references to Appendices
	Sept 29		Two telephone wires laid. Batteries in position shortly. Began 2 am. Casualties. Officers wounded 2. O.R. killed 5. wounded 30. gassed 5. missing 2. 8 guns out of action. Expended 120 rounds.	
	30		A & D Batteries registered.	

J.D. Dainier
Col.
Comm'd'g 94th Bde R.F.A.

121/7595

21st Division

9th Bav: R. Da.
Vol 2

Oct. 15

Army Form C. 2118.

WAR DIARY
or
INTELLIGENCE SUMMARY.
(Erase heading not required.)

Instructions regarding War Diaries and Intelligence Summaries are contained in F. S. Regs., Part II. and the Staff Manual respectively. Title pages will be prepared in manuscript.

Place	Date 1915	Hour	Summary of Events and Information	Remarks and references to Appendices
	Oct. 1		Two sections each of A and D Batteries returned by 6th Bde.	
	2		Batteries went (?) 30 rounds at "BOIS HUGO". Remaining sections relieved at 9 pm. marched to MAZINGARBE & bivouacked.	
	3		Marched 8½ miles & bivouacked.	
	4		Marched 5.30 am marched to NEUF BERQUIN & bivouacked.	
	5		Marched by HAZEBROUCK to STRAZEELE, horses and bullets great difficulty about [water]	
	6		Several sub-sections came in very good hrs. OC Indian wan activities for [illegible] promotion (for good) and plucky work.	
	7		Signal Keyston name [illegible] for [illegible] to [illegible].	
	8		Brig. Gen. Mulcahy-Morgan visited – several officers commanding batteries recommended for mention.	
	9		Maj. Gen. Jomba. Nother inspected Brigade and congratulated them on their Manner and Performance.	
	10			
	21		Sections of A, C & D Batteries marched to ARMENTIERES and replaced sections of 3rd Lahore Div. Brigade in firing line	
	22		August Ann. (Canine) marched into ARMENTIERES	
	23		Remaining sections marched to ARMENTIERES and supplied the section of the 3rd Jullundur Bde. B Battery remaining (with men and guns) but disposing on arrival of [illegible] in full near STRAZEELE	

Army Form C. 2118.

WAR DIARY
or
INTELLIGENCE SUMMARY.

(Erase heading not required.)

Place	Date	Hour	Summary of Events and Information	Remarks and references to Appendices
	Oct 30		G. Smith killed by enemy shell in front trench.	

94th Bde: R.F.A.
Vol: 3

121/7624

21st Known

Nov. 15.

Army Form C.2118.

WAR DIARY
or
INTELLIGENCE SUMMARY.
(Erase heading not required.)

Instructions regarding War Diaries and Intelligence Summaries are contained in F.S. Regs., Part II. and the Staff Manual respectively. Title pages will be prepared in manuscript.

Place	Date	Hour	Summary of Events and Information	Remarks and references to Appendices
ARMENTIERES	Nov. 1		Major R.E. Dyer admitted to Hospital	
			2/Lt. E.H. Fuller admitted to Hospital	
			2/Lt. P.W.A. Reid arrived temporary command of B/Battery	
	7		B/Battery marched from STRAZEELE to ARMENTIERES to take up position in the line.	
	8		Capt. M.R.C. Nanson joined and assumed command of B Battery	
	12		Lt. Marchant D. Battery, wounded by shrapnel	
	13		2/Lt. P.H.S. Boysudenhost, joined	
	(23		Lieut. H.A.B. Shirley & 2/Lt. C.J.F Mulet-Isale joined	
	18		Lt. Panes 110 Br Staff and Lt. Puget J. D Bty admitted hospital suffering from shock. result of bombardment of ARMENTIERES.	
	25		2/Lt. F.O. Freeman joined	
	30		Lt. Gibbins B/Bty wounded, Lt. Shattock injured from recoil of gun	

[signature]
Comdg 94th Br.Bde

21st Divisional Artillery.

94th BRIGADE R. F. A.

JANUARY 1916.

WAR DIARY
or
INTELLIGENCE SUMMARY.

Army Form C. 2118.

Place: ARMENTIERES

Date	Hour	Summary of Events and Information	Remarks and references to Appendices
1915	2	N° 76896 A/Bdr. O'Brien – wounded – sniped in trenches	
	3	B. Battery in position at CHAPELLE D'ARMENTIERES were heavily shelled. From 10.5 am and 8" and were used – men took refuge in support trenches and some in cellar of house close to position – the house was hit by an 8" shell which ahead and collapsed trenching in the roof of the cellar and burying officers and men resulting in the following casualties:— 2/Lt H.W. Jones slight wound; N° 36054 Gr Lt Cook, 55791 Gunner W. Savage, 63519 Gr W. Strutbridge, 89693 Gunner J. Medbury. Very little damage was done to equipment – Gunner 35058 Lt Hughes was hit by piece of shell which burst just outside N° 2 Gun and also taken in the day.	
	4	Capt. GEN. Franklyn went on leave	
	10	Major W.T. Dymott went on leave 18905 Gr. Hamden R.Bty. wounded by rifle burning rack of pieces which	
	11	A new entrance was arrived at by the 61st by Brigade at Pont BALLOT. Antwerks supported by Batteries of the Brigade. A Battery. Capt. Terry	Sheet 36 N.W. Corp: cx and

WAR DIARY
or
INTELLIGENCE SUMMARY.

(Erase heading not required.)

Army Form C. 2118.

84th BRIGADE
JAN 1916
ROYAL FIELD ARTILLERY

Place	Date Dec.	Hour	Summary of Events and Information	Remarks and references to Appendices
ARMENTIERES	5		B. Battery was off for one parting in right sector, and commenced the preparation of emplacements in Chapelle d'ARMENTIERES	
	6		1 section of B. Bty moved to new position	
	10		knowing section 7.B. Battery moved into new position, and the Battery came under the orders of the 90 & 96 gr Batt. for tactical purposes	
			No. 85549 Driver Mercam A - wounded by shell fire in ARMENTIERES	
			No. 99280 Driver B. Cummings - killed by shell fire in ARMENTIERES	
	14		No. 36235 Driver R. Pelham - severely wounded at same time and also one night	
			No. 37194 Driver R. Stocks admitted to hospital suffering from shock	
	16		No. 26210 Gunner Guy wounded	
	23		Capt. M.R.C. Warren proceeded on leave	
	24		Capt. W.C.L. Corry ,, ,,	
	30		2/Lt. G.E.T. Egerton ,, ,,	

Army Form C. 2118.

WAR DIARY
or
INTELLIGENCE SUMMARY.
(Erase heading not required.)

Place	Date	Hour	Summary of Events and Information	Remarks and references to Appendices
	11		directing the fire from front trenches - The arrival in the enemy trenches was marked at 11·15 pm a barrage of fire being made by A + D Batteries. 2 prisoners were captured. The barrament promptly completed the Battery commanders on their effective and accurate shooting in this barrage	
	16		Lieut A.P. Irvine proceeded on leave	
	21		Lieut R.T. Neil " "	
	23 24 26		Capt H.C. Long wounded by high burst over Battery position Capt. P. Mahoney went on leave 37159, Gr T.C. Blenter, 67980 Gr J. Hogarth both killed and 37181 Gr J. Wilkinson severely wounded by a shell bursting in C Bty position	
	29		The section of "B" Battery near L/S Farm was relieved by 10·5pm without 60 shells falling close to position, no damage to equipment	
	29 30		No 36009 Gr Turnbull wounded No 37415 Gr J. Paul wounded 37h P.V.A. Reid went on leave No 19099 Gunner W. Adcock awarded D.C.M.	J. Bromber Lt. Br 3. B J. B...L Qm (cons)

2353 Wt. W2514/1454 700,000 5/15 D. D. & L.   A.D.S.S./Form/C. 2118.

21st Divisional Artillery.

94th BRIGADE R. F. A.

FEBRUARY 1916.

WAR DIARY or INTELLIGENCE SUMMARY

Army Form C. 2118.

(Erase heading not required.)

Instructions regarding War Diaries and Intelligence Summaries are contained in F.S. Regs., Part II. and the Staff Manual respectively. Title pages will be prepared in manuscript.

Place: ARMENTIERES

Date	Hour	Summary of Events and Information	Remarks and references to Appendices
11	11.0	Minor Enterprise carried out against the Enemy's trenches in the PONT BALLOT SALIENT. Tasks allotted to B and D Btys this Brigade. No 30891 Gunner A. Nunn of D/91 wounded.	2nd DA 00.11 Sheet 36 N.W. C29 a c
12	4.30 pm	D Battery 113th Brigade (How) moved into Brigade area, placed under my command for tactical purposes. Battery commanded by Major Craw Heart.	
14		No 31666 Sgt. J. Henley and No 106193 Bdr W. Murphy both of B Bty wounded when repairing telephone wires.	2nd DA 6.0.14
15		Minor Enterprise with object to damage the Enemy's trenches and interfere with his Brigade & his works. D/113, A/91, B/91, How batteries & B/91, D/91 attacked trenches at PONT BALLOT SALIENT. Result was very good.	
		Registered bombardment of enemy's trenches at I.Sc.9.1.6, I.n.a.97.83 and I.Sc.9.2.3, K.15.A.h.1 and SPARROWS NEST I.SD.0.1 Trenches allotted to D/13 & B/91 How and A and C Btys this Brigade. Considerable damage done Enemy's works.	2nd DA 00.15 Sheet 36 N.W.
16		Further bombardment of Enemy's trenches along the front and communication trenches from I.S.9.4.3 northwards to C.29.a.15.1 + Batteries of this Brigade engaged in these B/91 and D/113 Hows. (BRUNE RUE Iss b c) A C & D Btys 91	2nd DA 6.0.14 Sheet 36 N.W.
19		Further bombardment of Enemy's support trenches and strong points in Rhenos & Rhenos. LE TEMPLE — L'AVENTURE, ARRET and LA TRESNELLE (B/91 How) other batteries employed B.O.D. 91 & other trenches	2nd DA 6.0.14 Sheet 36 N.W.
		D/113 Hows	

WAR DIARY or INTELLIGENCE SUMMARY

Army Form C. 2118.

Place: RANIE NTIERE S

Date	Hour	Summary of Events and Information	Remarks and references to Appendices
20 Feb		No 6366 Sr T H Dawson A Bty and No 97671 Dr Quinn of D/94 wounded. A cutting out expedition was organised preceded by a bombardment of Enemy's trenches at RAILWAY SALIENT (I 11 a) BLACK REDOUBT (I s c 9.1 & I s c 8 3). The point of entry for the attacking party from the 10th Yorks Regiment was at I s c 9s.2 s, the Enemy's wire at this point facing at by A Battery. The fire of the Battery was preventing the Enemy approaches from the trenches. The wire was successfully cut under cover approaching in account of unfavourable weather conditions and by the previous hostile attempt which was very active over our lines - the assault under cover of a 3 minutes' bombardment of the front trenches from 10.57 to 11 pm on that night, was made at 11pm, at which hour Batteries lifted their fire to form barrage against reinforcements being brought up from support - The front party of the assaulting party on reaching the enemy's wire was seen by the sentries and were bombed, and two officers were wounded, and the assaulting party returned from thence.	
26 Feb		Have received that D Bty 156 Brigade in repair 25th Division Artillery billeted that night in major lines was moved to CAESTRE on morning of 29th Feb.	

4/3/16   R Donnelly Lt. Col. Comdg N 94 R.F.A.

21st Divisional Artillery.

94th BRIGADE R. F. A.

MARCH 1916.

Army Form C. 2118.

WAR DIARY
or
INTELLIGENCE SUMMARY. 94th Brigade R.G.A.

(Erase heading not required.)

Instructions regarding War Diaries and Intelligence Summaries are contained in F. S. Regs., Part II. and the Staff Manual respectively. Title pages will be prepared in manuscript.

Place	Date	Hour	Summary of Events and Information	Remarks and references to Appendices
Ameetin	9		2/Lt. Hyde-Walters wounded slightly in leg by rifle bullet. A minor enterprise was carried out by trench mortars having as an objective the destroying of Farm B. Mortar machine gun experiments at PONT BRIOT SALIENT. Looks allotted to B & D Batteries to suppress enemy front support trenches during the bombardment by trench mortars. The results are good and a distance of about 8 yards was traded by Senior Mortars. Damages by Senior Mortars.	R/ Corres 2nd D.A. Trench Maps 0018
	15		The following wounded in A Bty. position. No 838?? Cpl Jones E.T. No 249158 Bdr Watson J.H. No 34461 A/Bdr Newman S. No 15703 Gr Scanlon J.	
	18		The Relief of the 2nd Div. commenced by the 17th Division. Section of B & D Btys returned on this date and marched to billet area in CAESTRE	Sheet 27
	19		Remaining sections of B & D/94 relieved by B & D 78 on this day	
	20		Brigade Ammunition Column relieved by BAC 78th Div.	
	22		Sections of A & C/94 relieved by section of A & C/78	
	23		Remaining sections of A & C relieved	
			Brigade ammunition recovered moved to CAESTRE	
CAESTRE			Motor gasoline moved to CAESTRE.	
	25		The Commander in Chief received the new and inspected the men and inspected the C & D Bty's dismounted who represent this subscription with their unit	2nd D.A. RO D/G 379
	25		The 2nd Army Commander inspected me battery of each Brigade	

Army Form C. 2118.

WAR DIARY
or
INTELLIGENCE SUMMARY.
(Erase heading not required.)

Instructions regarding War Diaries and Intelligence Summaries are contained in F. S. Regs., Part II. and the Staff Manual respectively. Title pages will be prepared in manuscript.

Place	Date	Hour	Summary of Events and Information	Remarks and references to Appendices
CAESTRE	28		A. By of 94 Bde proceeding. The 2nd Army Commander directs the G.O.C.R.A. 2nd Div. to army to all ranks of the Divisional Artillery his appreciation and thanks for the good work done by them during the past few months	
	29		The Division ordered to join XIII Corps	
	30		Batteries ammunition columns entrained at CASSELL and detraining at LONGEAU.	
	31		Brigade Staff and HQrs entrained, arriving at DAOURS on morning 1st April & billeting area at DAOURS	

J. Bannatyne Bne
Cmdg 94th Brigade R.F.A.

21st Divisional Artillery.

94th BRIGADE R. F. A.

APRIL 1916.

Army Form C. 2118.

XXI   Vol 8

96th Bde R.F.A.

WAR DIARY
or
INTELLIGENCE SUMMARY.
(Erase heading not required.)

Instructions regarding War Diaries and Intelligence Summaries are contained in F.S. Regs., Part II. and the Staff Manual, respectively. Title pages will be prepared in manuscript.

Place	Date	Hour	Summary of Events and Information	Remarks and references to Appendices
DAOURS	April 1		Detrained at 2 am at LONGEAU arriving at billets here at 6 am	Sheet 62D NE 1/40,000
MONT	8		A Battery relieved B Battery 165th Brigade 32nd Division at F.5c.7.2 taking over the guns of 1/B/165	
	9/10		Relieves of B.C. & D btys 96th Brigade relieved sections of F and T batteries 1st R.Bde R.H.A. at F.19.a.6.5 and F.19.a.4.5	
	10		Reorganising sections of B.C.D. Bty which relieved T and T batteries were completed by 8.30 pm. Reconnaissance commenced at this hour.	Sheet 57 D SE
	11		The first ranging by the Brigade firing from F.9.a.5.6 & X.30c.2.0 was taken up by C Battery 96th Brigade who opened action of 9th Divisional Artillery at F.9.a.1.9 remained tactically under my command. The 96th Brigade fired together with the heavy Artillery buttressed the General Defence arcs of fire in at intervals from 5.45 pm to 6.28 pm. The shooting was very good	
	29		The enemy bombarded the TAMBOUR and Trenches S. of it from 1am to 5 am. Heavy bombardment. Heavy fighting in trenches at 15h 5.45 am	
	30		At 2.10 am the enemy trench mortars on a front from the TAMBOUR to FORTHEET our Artillery opened fire at once and the enemy was put up very suddenly in a very short time. A considerable [?] [?] of the enemy entered our trenches leaving him prisoners in our hands	

Army 9.94. B.R.F.A. Jno Rainston Lt.

21st Divisional Artillery.

94th BRIGADE R. F. A.

M A Y 1916.

Army Form C. 2118.

WAR DIARY
or
INTELLIGENCE SUMMARY.
(Erase heading not required.)

Place	Date	Hour	Summary of Events and Information	Remarks and references to Appendices
MEAULTE (ALBERT)	April 30		At about 7.45 p.m. the enemy burst in a shell over BONTE REDOUBT and also bombarded our trenches. Our Batteries immediately opened a fast rate of fire. A rate of about 600 rounds per hour. The enemy infantry made no attempt to cross over their trenches however and all was quiet at 9 p.m. The Brigade had two casualties from gas. 1 Officer and B.O.R.	
Do	May 3		2/Lt. E.S. Davis was sent up to D Battery from Armn. Rft. to replace Lt. Hume admitted to hospital	
	5		In pursuance of 30/4/16 2/Lt. G.R.H. Wallace which H.Q. the strength dwindled to England 2/Lt. H.M. Jones " " " " failed to return to France Maj. H.R.C. Harris " " went on leave.	
	8		Lt. F.M. Bennett Cmdg. Brigade went on leave, Major W.T. Symcott took over command of Brigade	
	9		Col E. Pottinger 9) " F.A. Bde took over command of Gp. in the absence of Col Bennett	
	6			
	8		At about 5h B Battery position came in for a very heavy shell which caused some damage in communication No. 5 & 6 Bh P. Lefts. N.C. being killed.	
	10			

WAR DIARY

INTELLIGENCE SUMMARY.

Place	Date	Hour	Summary of Events and Information	Remarks and references to Appendices
MEAULTE	1/6		A raid on the enemies trenches was attempted at 2 a.m by 1st Somerset L.I. An artillery barrage was to have formed unless ordered [?] no artillery [?] fire. The raid was not successful and by our own regiment.	
	20		Brigades was altered. B. Bty /94 ('18 pr) became formation of Brigades was altered. B. Bty 97th Bde (How) became D/94 (How) [?] B/97 Bde RFA. Then the Brigade is composed of three 18 pr Batteries and one How (4.5") Battery. ※ D.Bty 94t Bde ('18 pr) became B/94. ('18 pr) ※ 97 Bde (How) joined from 97 R FA Bde. The following officers Major H.G. Boon His Collins Lieut [?] B. Mulholland " E.C. Brooks 2/Lt [?] [?] heat. The following officers quitted the 94t F. Bde and joined 97t Bde Major M.R.C. haron Lieut P.A.V. Reid P.H.S. Byzandern-Lint B.J. Kambetee J [?]	

3/6/16

Army Form C. 2118.

WAR DIARY
or
INTELLIGENCE SUMMARY. Copy
(Erase heading not required.)

Place	Date	Hour	Summary of Events and Information	Remarks and references to Appendices
MEAULTE	May 27/28		B & C Batteries of this Brigade relieved by batteries of the 96th Brigade.	
	29"		Col Fitzgerald assumed command of the Group. "A" Battery and "D" Battery (Howitzers) remaining in their original positions and coming under that command.	

To D.A.G. 3rd Echelon

War diary A.F.C 2118 for
May of 94th Bde R.F.A. is
forwarded herewith

3/6/16

Tv Brewster (?)
Comd 94 Bde

21st Divisional Artillery.

94th BRIGADE R. F. A.

JUNE 1916.

JUNE
Vol 10

WAR DIARY
or
INTELLIGENCE SUMMARY.

94th Bde R.G.A.

Army Form C. 2118.

(Erase heading not required.)

Place	Date	Hour	Summary of Events and Information	Remarks and references to Appendices
MEAULTE	May 27/18		B & C Batteries of this Brigade relieved by Batteries of the 95th Brigade	
"	29		The 94th Bgde assumed command of the group. A Battery and D Battery (Howitzer) remaining in their original positions and coming under this Command	
"	June 13		D Battery suffered the following casualties from a premature round. N° 63506 Bdr Appleyard (killed) 55416 Bdr Hannon N° 84094 Gr. the following N° 46636 Gr. Taylor, N° 111181 Gr. Downs N° 49126 Gr. Edwards N° 51555 Gr. Hannon N° 63798 Gr. Mackinnon (all wounded) N° 37026 Gr. J. Dixon of A. Bty. killed by machine gun fire when preparing forward position	
"	14		B & C Batteries moved to new acting positions at E.12.a.3.9 + E.11.d.3.3 close to BECORDEL	Sheet 57 SE
"	23		A. B. & C. Batteries of 94th Bde R.G.A. placed under my technical Command and took up following positions. A Bty (Capt. Jones.) F.24.7.1 B Bty (Major Shannon) F.24.7.3 - C Bty (Major Raven) F.20.a.0.3	

Army Form C. 2118.

WAR DIARY
or
INTELLIGENCE SUMMARY.   94 A.Bde R.F.A

(Erase heading not required.)

Place	Date	Hour	Summary of Events and Information	Remarks and references to Appendices
	June 24th	3.30 am	Preliminary bombardment + wire cutting for the attack commenced	21st D.A. Instructions for Offence No. 3. 15/6/16
			Brigade Zone for wire cutting:-	
			F3a 9.1 to X27a 0.0	
			F3a 9.8 to F3a 6.6.7	
			F3a 6.0.5 to X27c 5.5.5.0	
			F3d 20.6.5 to X27c 6.7	
			X29c 10.4.5 to X28c 0.8	
			F3c 6.5.90 to X27c 40.1.5	
			Gun line	
			The whole zone allotted to Brigade is	
			a line F3c 6590 - F3a 9.8 - X28d 82 - X30a 0560 and	MONTAUBAN Trench map 1/10000
			a line X27c 4015 - X28c 2.9 (Peicourt Farm inclusive) - X28d 3.1 (Railway	
			Copse inclusive) - X23d 4.0	
25 to 30th			Wire cutting + bombardment of enemy defences continued as laid down in 21st D.A. Instructions for Offence No. 3 of 15/6/16 in above mentioned zone.	

Casualties of 3rd June

Nil. Bdr Sampson of HQ Bos } Honours
Nil. Bdr Liale of B Bty } Military medal

[signature]
R.D. Birchur ?
Major ? 94th BJRFA

21st DA

War Diary

I beg to forward the above for month of July 1916

1/8/16

A P Sumner
Lieut
for OC 94th DA Bde

21st **Divisional Artillery.**

94th **BRIGADE R. F. A.**

J U L Y 1916.

Army Form C. 2118.

WAR DIARY
or
INTELLIGENCE SUMMARY. 94th Bde R.F.A.   Vol 1/6
(Erase heading not required.)

July 1916

Instructions regarding War Diaries and Intelligence Summaries are contained in F. S. Regs., Part II. and the Staff Manual respectively. Title pages will be prepared in manuscript.

Place	Date	Hour	Summary of Events and Information	Remarks and references to Appendices
BECORDEL	1	am 6.25	The commencement of concentrated bombardment in accordance with 21st DA Instructions for Offence Nº U	All map references in MONTAUBAN & MARTINPUICH Trench Maps 1/10000
		7.30	Enemy front line attacked by 63rd & 64th Infantry Brigades and the 50th Brigade (17th Div) to clear front system of enemy trenches on right flank of assaulting troops and to occupy position in neighbourhood of Red Cottage	
		pm 2.30	Attack on FRICOURT which was preceded by bombardment for 30 minutes. The attack was held up by machine guns in craters.	
	2		A further attack on FRICOURT was timed for 13 noon, to be preceded by bombardment, but as men were reported as being seen to leave trenches, and the orders for bombardment were cancelled. Brigade ordered to barrage from F11 a 0550 along tracks running to FRICOURT FARM. Infantry advanced and encountered no opposition.	
		pm 1.10	Own Infantry reported on a line from X28 c 1.0 to POODLES	
		pm 1.15	A.Bty. ordered to move up to BECORDEL and have plenty of other batteries to another position. O/C A-Bty. reconnoitred position in X27 a	
		pm 9.15	Orders received for A.Bty. to return to BELLE VUE FARM and harness of other batteries to wagon lines.	

Army Form C. 2118.

WAR DIARY
or
INTELLIGENCE SUMMARY.
(Erase heading not required.)

94th Bde R.F.A.

July 1916

Place	Date	Hour	Summary of Events and Information	Remarks and references to Appendices
	3	9 am	A. Bty ordered up to BECORDEL VILLAGE. O/C of Battery Commander reconnoitred position near DUNKEN ROAD and reported attack not sufficiently advanced to allow of Battery being taken up	
	4	pm 8.15	A. Bty moved up into forward position at X 27 d.2.1. A Bty in action registered. Casualties. Gunners N° 82991 G. Morris A.Bty - N° 86698 Bdr Swindles C.Bty. wounded N° 34541 Sgt Brunkill. C. Bty.	
			Battery positions reconnoitred remaining batteries in X 27 d and F5 a Casualties wounded N° 34541 Sgt Brunkill C Bty	
	5	am 9.45	Orders to remove CONTALMAISON at slow rate of fire for 30 minutes B.C.D. Btys gu. and A+C Btys 79 rounds turned on Col. Earth	21st D.A. M B 407
		1 pm	Batteries of 79th Bde passed to command of 94th Bde	M B 413
		10 pm	Orders for night firing - CONTALMAISON and BEZENTIN-le-PETIT. Batteries did not fire.	
	6		Casualties. Shell shock N° 63607 Gr. Batey A Bty	
	7	2 am	5th Brigade attacks on PEAR+ALLEY. Tasks allotted to Batteries	2nd D.A. D.O. 23
		1.25 & 2 am	Harass trench running West of CONTALMAISON X 16 d.5.1.k X 16 b.1.4	

Army Form C. 2118.

WAR DIARY
or
INTELLIGENCE SUMMARY.
(Erase heading not required.)

July 1914 94 A Bde. R.F.A. 3

Place	Date	Hour	Summary of Events and Information	Remarks and references to Appendices
9	7	7-3 am	Reports attack failed, and orders to carry out Bombardment as laid down in para 7 of O.O. 24.	
		5 pm	Attack on QUADRANGLE SUPPORT. TRENCH - ACID DROP COPSE - Strips of WOOD between WOOD TRENCH & WOOD SUPPORT. Orders for bombardment at 7.30 pm as laid down in BM 472.	2nd DA BM 472
	8	5.50 pm	Attacks on flanks of QUADRANGLE SUPPORT and junction of PEARL ALLEY and junction of PEARL ALLEY & QUADRANGLE SUPPORT. Tasks of Btys. A. MIDDLE ALLEY - D Bty. WOOD TRENCH	2nd DA O.O. 25
	9	2 pm	Enemy shells heavily from N. of SHELTER WOOD & OVILLERS and trenches from BOTTOM WOOD to QUADRANGLE. Orders 2 batteries in to WOOD TRENCH SUPPORTS	
	10	3.30 am	Bombardment of Southern & South West portion of MAMETZ WOOD. Tasks as laid down in 21st DA O.O. 29. 10/7/16	21st DA O.O. 27 10/7/16
		11 pm	Batteries of Brigade ordered to occupy forward positions - The approach was being shelled along SUNKEN ROAD - C Bty dropped into position. Between LOZENGE WOOD & LONELY COPSE - B Bty returned to original position A & C Batteries from former position also were sending on front S.13.d.7.7 & S.13.d.4.9	
	11			

Army Form C. 2118.

WAR DIARY
or
INTELLIGENCE SUMMARY.

9th H.Bde. R.G.A.

July 1916

(Erase heading not required.)

Place	Date	Hour	Summary of Events and Information	Remarks and references to Appendices
	11		Batteries took up forward positions during the night. R.S.C. along ledge running from SHELTER WOOD & BOTTOM WOOD in X.26.d. - D.Bty at T.5.a. 3.8.	
			Casualties 10th H.Q. gunner Sgt Porter. A.Bty - No 35534 Gr Tavin. A.Bty wounded. 11th No 34814 Bdr Jordan . C.Bty. No 56176 Sgt Myers C.Bty ,	
	12	2am 10.30	Men resting from S.13.d.7.7. & S.13.d.4.9. and zone rept under fire during night. Concentrated bombardment on BAZENTIN-le-PETIT WOOD for 5 minutes. Casualties Killed No 63570 Gr Breggatt B.Bty. - No 68004 Gr Stepney C.Bty. No 101039 Gr Campbell C.Bty. No 119475 Gr Stoneel C.Bty. Wounded No 101039 Gr Campbell C.Bty. continued	
	13.		Bombardment of above zone S.13.d.7.7. & S.13.d.4.9. BAZENTIN-le-PETIT WOOD.	
	14.	am 3.70 3.25	Attack on BAZENTIN-le-PETIT WOOD. Bombardment of front line Barrage lifted and infantry attacked Barrages lifted as rain down in operation order.	2nd D.A. O.O. 27
		pm 12.35	Attack successful through taken inward to fire continual bursts of fire 300 yds clear of N.W. corner of B-le-P. Wood.	

Army Form C. 2118.

WAR DIARY
or
INTELLIGENCE SUMMARY.
(Erase heading not required.)

Place	Date	Hour	Summary of Events and Information	Remarks and references to Appendices
	14		Night firing on Agenue M 32. Casualties wounded. N° 36585 Bdr Bishop. B. Bty. N° 111313 Gr Walker. B. Bty. N° 55615 Gr Gray B. Bty. N° 34635 Gr Petersham B. Bty. N° 9910 Gr Scruggs. D. Bty.	2nd D.A. M.B. 63v
	15	11.7 am	Barrage 30 yds clear of N.W. edge of B.L.-P. Wood. own fire 3 rises. Believed to kill Rly from S8a 1260 to S2c.1040, with A.B.C. Btys and D Bty engage enemy guns reported at S8a N.6.	M B 638
		1.55	Above order cancelled.	
		1.48 pm	Night firing as this down in MB 662. Southern boundary of Zone S1d 58 to S2c 0.8. Casualties N° 94294 Bdr Craven C Bty. N° 120379 Gr Hostel C. Bty. both wounded.	
	16	10 am	Believed to search for mine in front of Switch Trench S.1.t.5.1 to S2c.10.15. Night firing same. Casualties wounded. N° 36590 Bdr Boyle B. Bty. N° 34590 Gr Mouser B. Bty. N° 36033 Gr Lavin B. Bty. N° 26398 Gr Hogg A. Bty.	
	17		Bursts of fire during day. enemy in Switch Trench Casualties wounded N° 47170 Dr McDonnell. D Bty.	
	18/19		As on previous day.	

WAR DIARY
or
INTELLIGENCE SUMMARY.
(Erase heading not required.)

Army Form C. 2118.

Place	Date	Hour	Summary of Events and Information	Remarks and references to Appendices
	20	am 2.55	Bombarded SWITCH TRENCH from S2 d 4.6 to M33 c 0.0 & M33 c 0.0 to M33 d 2.5.0, in support of attacks by XV and XIII Corps. Fire continued up to 4.75 am	2nd D.A. from XIII Corps O.O. 29
	21	am 6 am 3.70 3.30	Night firing on SWITCH TRENCH. S2 d 4.6 to M33 c 0.0 by A.B.C. S2 c 038 to S2 d 4.6 - D Bty. Casualties Wounded 1 Rk N.C.O. Prisoner A.T. Bty. N° 1179 G.S. Lewis C Bty. Night firing as on previous night. Concentrated bombardment on SWITCH TRENCH - M33 d r 1.5 to M33 c 7.3	2nd D.A. O.O. 30
	22	7 am to 1.30	Commencement of bombardment on Zone S2 L 6085 to M33 d 5505 in support of attack by XIII Corps on DELVILLE WOOD - III Corps on SWITCH TRENCH on the left of XV Corps at this time. Night firing M33 d 6.0 to S2 a 0.7	2nd D.A. O.O. 31
	23		Brigade withdrawn from the line and marches to BONNAY	
	24 25 26		Continued move to ARGOEUVES	
	27		" " BOURDON	
	29		" " ST. RIQUIER	
	30		" " BEALCOURT	
			" " LIGNY-SUR-CANCHE	

21st Divisional Artillery.

94th BRIGADE R. F. A.

AUGUST 1916.

WAR DIARY
INTELLIGENCE SUMMARY.

94th Brigade R.F.A.

August

Place	Date	Hour	Summary of Events and Information	Remarks and references to Appendices
	July 31st		Gr. W. Riley No. 36559 of C.Bty awarded Military Medal.	
	Aug 1st		Orders received for the relief of 14th Divisional Artillery. This Brigade relieves 46th Brigade.	Trench Map ARRAS 51 B NW 3
	2nd		The O.C. and Recce August Officers went to H.Q. of 46th Bde. Batteries of the following batteries relieved sections of 46th Bdr as follows:— A relieves A/46 at G 15 d 3.0 B " B/46 " G 21 a 5.5 C (1 Battn) C/46 one gun at G 15 d 8.3 C (1 gun) C/46 one gun " G 21 b 9.8 D relieves D/46 at G 15 d 5.5.6. The following places under this Brigade for tactical purposes. 9u7 relieves 9u8 at G 15 a 7505 9u9 one gun at G 29 c 3.4 (1dco) B/97 (1 gun)	
	3		Headquarters of Brigade and remaining sections of above batteries relieves remaining sections of 46th Brigade — Relief completed by 12.30 am morning of 3rd.	

WAR DIARY
or
INTELLIGENCE SUMMARY.
(Erase heading not required.)

Army Form C. 2118.

Place	Date	Hour	Summary of Events and Information	Remarks and references to Appendices
	8		Line held by Infantry as follows:- Sector J₁ by 63rd Inf Brigade trenches 81 to 93. Sector J₂ by 110th Inf Brigade trenches 94 to 101.	Trench map Arras 51ᵇ NW 3
	14		Batteries of the Group arrived at scenes of concentration.	
	15		Instruments in Hqd 65ᵗʰ⁵ and Hqd 7.2. Divisional Commander visited batteries at 5am. Divisional Commander visited wagon lines of Batteries following morning. Military medals.	
			N° 24719 Sgt G.W. Yeoman D Bty
			8x681 Gr. I.J. Cooper A13Bty
			83995 Gr. E. Peters A13Bty
			63814 Dr. G.E. Davis A13Bty
	16		2ⁿᵈ D.A. O.O. 1 received regarding the re-organising of the front by 124ᵗʰ Inf Bde RGA. 37ᵗʰ Div.	
	18		Sections of above Brigade moved into positions as follows:	
			A G 15 a 7.0 C G 15 d 3.7	
			B G 28 a 1.1 D G 15 a 5.1	

WAR DIARY
or
INTELLIGENCE SUMMARY.
(Erase heading not required.)

Army Form C. 2118.

Place	Date	Hour	Summary of Events and Information	Remarks and references to Appendices
	18/19		The section of A/m relieved section of C/97 covering trenches S8-9v	
	19/20		The remaining sections of 10th Brigade came into action and remaining sections of C/97 relieved by sections of A/10	
	20/21 Wed		Minor operation carried out in accordance with 2nd Div Arty O.O. & C.18 a 21 and C.12 a 30 9s Wire firing out during 2300 & 2330. at C.18 a 21 and C.12 a 30 9s Enemy trenches at C.12 a 35 9s covered by barrage fire from batteries of the Brigade Front The enemy party found enemy trenche empty and all the party returned.	2nd D.A. C.O. No. 2
	21	9 pm	No 47126 a/Bor Connor D1 Bty wounded by premature	

R. Bamither Col
Comdg 97 F.A.Bde

21st Divisional Artillery.

94th BRIGADE R. F. A.

SEPTEMBER 1916.

WAR DIARY or INTELLIGENCE SUMMARY

Army Form C. 2118.

September 1916. 94th Brigade R.F.A. Vol 13

Place	Date Sept	Hour	Summary of Events and Information	Remarks and references to Appendices
ARRAS	3		Col. The Branston to 50th D.A. during absence of Brig. R.A. on leave. Col. Knox resumed command of 94th Bde Group.	
	8		Orders received for the relief of the Brigade by the 159th B.A. Bde.	
	9		Col. Branston returned from D.A.	
	10		Sections of Batteries relieved by sections of 159th Bde and marched to ETREE-WAMIN. Relief of Brigade completed by 10.30 pm and remaining sections of Btys & HQ Bde marched to ETREE-WAMIN.	
	14		Brigade marches to SARTON and bivouacs the night.	
	13		Bivouacs marched arriving at BELLEVUE FARM at 11.30 pm. Batteries went into action on Square S.16 during night & Btteries in MONTAUBAN.	Sheet 57c SW. Morvae
	14		Registration carried out. 4th D.A. Order No.10 received for the attack on 15th inst. Objective Capturing defences to up and including the Line MORVAL - LES BOEUFS - GUEDECOURT and HIGH WOOD.	41st Div. Order 1849
	15	6.20	Zero hour of attack - The attack on Divisional front turned out very well. Captured Brigade on right and 15th Inf Bde on left - 123rd Inf Brigade in Reserve.	

Army Form C. 2118.

WAR DIARY
or
INTELLIGENCE SUMMARY.

(Erase heading not required.)

Instructions regarding War Diaries and Intelligence Summaries are contained in F. S. Regs., Part II. and the Staff Manual respectively. Title pages will be prepared in manuscript.

Place	Date	Hour	Summary of Events and Information	Remarks and references to Appendices
BN HQ BAN	15		Attack progressed well and at 3.28 p.m. the situation was reported as follows. Have approached to near N. of COURCELETTE – N. of MARTINPUICH down to High Wood (some firing still in High Wood) – Line thro' N. of M35 central to M36 central – FLERS has evacuated – FLERS situation obscure patrols were sent. – Our troops appear to have advanced from FB central. Tanks first employed on this day – Proved to be a success	H⁴ᵗʰ DB. Tr 6
	16		Attack continued on GIRD TRENCH & GIRD SUPPORTS in front of GUEDECOURT this was not successful and the line held on morning of the 17th on FLERS front was	
	17	4.40	Heavy rain & fog until 9 a.m. – Preliminary reconnaissance approved by Brigade during night on S15 C and d. Hrs. S18 a 15 Registration carried out at GIRD TRENCH	
	18		Day mostly firing trenches.	
	25	D.33	Attack on GIRD TRENCH & SUPPORTS & GUEDECOURT. GIRD TRENCH & SUPPORTS – Infantry gained GIRD TRENCH & SUPPORTS but did not establish themselves in GUEDECOURT.	H⁴ᵗʰ DA G.O. 17

Army Form C. 2118.

WAR DIARY
or
INTELLIGENCE SUMMARY.
(Erase heading not required.)

Place	Date	Hour	Summary of Events and Information	Remarks and references to Appendices
	7th/10	5.30	Attack on QUEDECOURT resumed, where we taken and consolidated during the day.	
	5"	7.15	B IRD TRENCH SUPPORTS from N76a 5.9 to N19b 3.7 attacked - objective gained. B Bhy & D Bhy actions formed to neutralise hostile new TREES in S6 and T1a respectively. (Carried out May night firing as ordered)	
	14/30			

[Signature]
Lt Col
Comd Th. RFA RFA
16/10/16

Army Form C. 2118.

94th A Bde
Sept/1916
Casualties

WAR DIARY or INTELLIGENCE SUMMARY.

(Erase heading not required.)

Place	Date	Hour	Summary of Events and Information	Remarks and references to Appendices
	14/9/16		No 109416 Gnr. Martin A. A Bty 94th Bde R.F.A. wounded in action	
	"		18969 Bgdr. Burbitt R. " " " Killed " "	
	"		66166 Cpl. Gordon H. " " " wounded " "	
	"		26927 Gnr. Richardson G. " " " Killed " "	
	"		82703 Bdr. Batley P. " " " Killed " "	
	"		19877 Gnr. Airey J. " " " wounded " "	
	"		18931 Sgt. Laenoe E. " " " " " remained at duty	
	"		128504 Gnr. Brundish W. " " " " " " "	
	"		9296 Gnr. Lowndes T.E. " " " " " " "	
	"		63661 Bdr. Bonfrey G. C Bty " " " "	
	15/9/16		25198 Sgt. Turner J.H. " " " Killed " "	
	"		63647 Gnr. Winter J.H. " " " wounded " "	
	"		77750 Gnr. Dodd R. " " " " "	
	"		22364 Gnr. Robson W. " " " " "	
	16/9/16		2/L. Dickman J.O. A Bty " " " Killed " "	
	17/9/16		47171 Gnr. Thompson W. B Bty " " " wounded " "	
	"		47256 Gnr. Wilson A.S. " " " " "	
	"		46676 Fitter Martin H. " " " " "	
	"		47275 Gnr. Barnard J. " " " " "	
	"		67605 Gnr. Rynnon A. " " " " "	
	"		63804 Gnr. Ellis W. " " " " "	
	"		63975 Gnr. Remington J. " " " " "	
	"		143042 Bdr. Hunter G.A. " " " " "	

Army Form C. 2118.

WAR DIARY
or
INTELLIGENCE SUMMARY.
(Erase heading not required.)

Instructions regarding War Diaries and Intelligence Summaries are contained in F.S. Regs., Part II. and the Staff Manual respectively. Title pages will be prepared in manuscript.

Place	Date	Hour	Summary of Events and Information	Remarks and references to Appendices
	17/9/16		2/Lt. Malet Veale C.J.J. "C" Bty. A/175 Bde. Bty. Col. R.F.A. wounded in action	
	18/9/16		No. 63626 Lnr. Lyman F. "A" Bty. " " " Killed	
			92945 Gnr. Peters E. " " " wounded	
	19/9/16		128504 Gnr. Brentnall W. " " " "	
			87599 Gnr. Smith R.S. "C" Bty. " " "	
			2/Lt. Weal L. " " " "	
	20/9/16		30474 Gnr. Gibson Wm. "D" Bty. " " "	
	25/9/16		50036 Gnr. Lewis J. " " " "	
	" "		63805 Gnr. Armstrong H. D/175 Bty " "	
	" "		34915 Gnr. Kearey J. "C" Bty. " "	
	" "		10376 Gnr. Martin S. "B"/154 " "	
	" "		45593 Bdr. Powell S. "C" Bty./154 " "	
	" "		Lt. Muller J.R. " " "	(accid. self inflicted)
	" "		2/Lt. Drew F.S. " " "	slight, remained at duty.
	26/9/16		34836 Gnr. John T.J. " " "	
	" "		96750 Gnr. Thomas J. " " "	
	25/9/16		83994 Bdr. Rood J. "D" Bty " "	
	28/9/16		46675 Dr. Wilson G. " " " Killed	
	" "		83988 Gnr. Gunnett T. " " " wounded	
	27/9/16		9922 Dr. Renwick H. "A" Bty " "	
	20/9/16		37229 Gnr. Burdy S.T. "B" Bty " "	

Wm. Snowden Col.
Comd.g. 175 B.D.G.
10/10/16

21st Divisional Artillery.

94th BRIGADE R. F. A.

OCTOBER 1916.

WAR DIARY or INTELLIGENCE SUMMARY

Army Form C. 2118.

Gurkha Brigade RFA
Chapter
Vol III
1916

(Erase heading not required.)

Date	Hour	Summary of Events and Information	Remarks and references to Appendices
1	AM 3.15	The New Zealand Division attacked the GIRD LINE on four on MEADOWS and Front running from that point to M.23.d.7.3 which was preceded by heavy bombardment along Divisional front. Bank Gp. Brigade K Barrage 250 x in front of First line GIRD SUPPORTS from N.19.b.5.5.5 to N.19.a.6.5.5	2nd DA to M.9 c.1
	Noon	A & C Batteries moved to forward positions near FLERS - A in SLL C in N.31.C.	
	9.15	Enemy reported massing for counter attack - intense barrage rate of fire for 30 minutes - attack did not develop - had heavy casualties not known	
		3rd Divn M.13.c.5.1. K M.13.a.5.1 - Enemy reported massing about E Tn line M.13.c.5.1 K.M.13.a.5.1 - Rapid fire 50 rounds per horn along a	
2	PM 12.30	rapid firing - DOS Line N.25.b.3 K N.13.c.3 K M.7.d.2.1.9 & M.13.C.0 & M.13.d.5.3	
3	8 pm	Generally a quiet day - Day Troops firing barrages met Reasons was that Division on left had all FAUCOURT ABBEY Ben Headquarters moved K FLARE TRENCH in SIR.K	2nd DA DHS

WAR DIARY or INTELLIGENCE SUMMARY

Army Form C. 2118.

Unit: October 1916 Gurkha Brigade RSR

Place	Date	Hour	Summary of Events and Information	Remarks and references to Appendices
Sq M 15	4	12.40	Enemy heavily barraged our trenches at Sunken Road in N94 - Ratlieu	
		11.35	Moved RHQ to LBS lines	
			Enemy barrage stopped	
		5.0	Enemy put up several SOS rockets. Batteries ordered to open fire again	
		5.40	Shelling stopped	
		6.30	Enemy shelled heavily N of COUSECOURT	
	5		Batteries slung kept up firing carried out.	
			Counted positions were shelled by 5.9's and 4.5 - Antenhouseus held to withdraw (Casualties 3 killed 5 wounded OR)	
	6	3.15 pm	Commencement of Bombardment in conjunction with 20 N's	21st Div OO N°5
	7	1.15 am	Infantry attack with objective BROWN LINE - Infantry advanced to the ridge but were held up by machine gun fire from right flank	
			Situation remained very obscure all day, but in the late evening defenders were reported 300 yards in front of original line	
			Enemy shell fire continued	
	8	am 7.15	Our guns continued Night 4.6 + N19 + 5 - 9 - M30 w.o	
		9.15		M30 w.o + M24 + 7 k

WAR DIARY
or INTELLIGENCE SUMMARY

Army Form C. 2118.

Oct 1/2 19 94th Brigade R.F.A.

Place	Date	Hour	Summary of Events and Information	Remarks and references to Appendices
	9	6pm 6.10	Batteries shelled trenches in front all day. Enemy put up heavy barrage along whole front - Batteries ordered to open fire in SOS lines - no attacks came - SOS answer/shots had improved	
		6.30	The barrage died away	
	10	6pm 12.40	Enemy day & night firing (Lines) out. June Alley reported full of Germans - all Batteries turned on this	
	11	7am	Bombardment of enemy trenches commenced in accordance with OO No 6 - BAYONET TRENCH - JUICE ALLEY - LIME TRENCH C/Bh, Batty shelled and had to withdraw from position and took up new position about S.6.d.8.1 (Casualties 2 killed and wounded 8 O.R.)	2nd D.A. OO N6L
	12	p. 3.5	Infantry attack with objective BROWN LINE - Objectives taken & gained. Orders for the Relief of 2nd Div Arty by 19th Div arty received	2nd D.A OO No 7 2nd DA [illegible] Relief N° 1
	13		Desultory day firing carried out	
	14	p. 8.30	Relief of A & B & D 94th retired by section of A.10 & D/61 R.F.A and section of A/114 Brigade & B/96 and moved to wagon lines. Remaining batteries relieved and Brigade Hqrs. R.F.A.	

WAR DIARY
or
INTELLIGENCE SUMMARY
(Erase heading not required.)

Army Form C. 2118.

94th Brigade R.F.A.

October 1916.

Place	Date	Hour	Summary of Events and Information	Remarks and references to Appendices
	15		Batteries relieved in proper night and 113 Bde war handed to Bombay and proved not fit [for] situations [who] handed in previous day.	
	16		Brigade marches to TALMAS (bivouac) for night	
	17		marches to AMPLIER	
	18		marches to BOUBERS-SUR-CANCHE	
	19		marches to BERGUENEUSE and EQUIRRE	
	20		marches to LAPUGNOY	
	21		The situation at [?] positions worried to wagon lines of battery of US the R.F.A. and relieves sections of Batteries that Brigade that night. A Bty & D Bty BM. B Bty and 2nd Bty. C Bty and 1/2 Bty - D Bty and 3rd Bty. Remaining sections marched to wagon lines and relieves remaining sections of above batteries next evening.	
	22		Command of front Quarries Sector have been taken over by O.C. 94th	

29/6/16
W. Hyland Major
Comdg 94th Bgde
RFA

WAR DIARY or INTELLIGENCE SUMMARY

Army Form C. 2118.

October 1916   G/HB/L/RFA

Place	Date	Hour	Summary of Events and Information			Remarks and references to Appendices
Field	1/10/16	—	Gr.	47257	Knapp. E.B.	D/21 Wounded In Action
" "	2/10/16	—	Sgt.	64672	Lawrence. J.A.C.	A/21 " " "
" "	" "	—	Gnr.	145343	Brennan J.G.	A/21 " " "
" "	" "	—	Gr.	63811	Cocker J.	B/21 " " "
" "	" "	—	Gr.	18476	Kaytzer J.	B/21 Wounded " "
" "	" "	—	Gr.	10963	Thompson A.J.	B/21 " " "
" "	" "	—	Br.	63687	Lemston. G	13/21 " " "
" "	" "	—	Lt.		Mulholland B.	D/21 " " "
" "	" "	—	Gnr.	89963	Longman a	M/21 Killed
" "	" "	—	Sgt.	46506	Crichwood. R.	D/21 " " "
" "	" "	—	Gr.	46661	McMurrimey	D/21 " " "
" "	" "	—	Gr.	47182	Wallace. G.	D/21 Wounded " "
" "	" "	—	Gr.	47805	Harmon. A.	D/21 " " "
" "	" "	—	Gr.	110625	Bennett. H.	D/21 " " "
" "	" "	—	Gr.	138557	Morgan. G.	D/21 " " "
" "	" "	—	Mr.	47158	Taylor A.G.	D/21 " " "
" "	3/10/16	—	Gr.	84775	Cuddy B.	B/21 Admitted to hospital with bruised leg.
" "	4/10/16	—	Bdr.	36184	Harding J.	A/21 Wounded In Action
" "	" "	—	Pte.	39424	Budge B.	C/21 " " "
" "	" "	—	Mr.	65849	Birdsall B.	C/21 " " "
" "	" "	—	Br.	46631	Elman	D/21 " " "
" "	5/10/16	—	Br.	26020	Loniston	A/21 " " "
" "	" "	—	Gr.	160901	Roy J. B.	B/21 " " "

Army Form C. 2118.

WAR DIARY
or
INTELLIGENCE SUMMARY.

(Erase heading not required.)

October 1916   Quebec Regt

Place	Date	Hour	Summary of Events and Information	Remarks and references to Appendices
Pic Co	3/10/16	—	CONTINUED	
"	"	—	115695 Pt. Rutherford A/9u Reported missing on the 6/10/16	
"	"	—	23390 Pr. Glen W. C/9u Killed in Action	
"	"	—	107651 Pr. Hawke E. C/9u " " "	
"	"	—	65475 Pr. Miller A.H. C/9u " " "	
"	"	—	37197 Pr. Knox J. C/9u Wounded	
"	"	—	P380r Sgt. Bird A. 9/9u " " "	
"	"	—	34762 Pr. Coleman J. C/9u " " "	
"	"	—	107900 Pr. Robinson J. C/9u Killed	
"	"	—	70750 Pr. Sheehan J.H. C/9u Wounded	
"	6/10/16	—	34161 Sgt. Nicholson P. A/9u Killed	
"	"	—	26162 Pr. Place J.W.J. A/9u Wounded	
"	"	—	26800 Cpl. Nicholson C. A/9u "	
"	10/10/16	—	34765 Pr. Underwood R. A/9u Wounded. In Action and remaining on Duty	
"	"	—	36279 Pr. Gibbons W. A/9u " " " "	
"	"	—	24664 Pr. Dayton J.H. C/9u " " " "	
"	"	—	73976 Sgt. Browne E. A/9u " " " "	
"	11/10/16	—	555737 Pr. Hurren J.H. B/9u Killed	
"	"	—	37169 Pr. Paterson J.R. C/9u Wounded	
"	"	—	4826s Sgt. Haskell S.W. C/9u Reported missing on the 11/10/16	
"	"	—	70548 Pr. Dempsey R. C/9u Killed in Action	
"	"	—	83002 Pr. Shorton W.E. C/9u Wounded " " "	

Army Form C. 2118.

WAR DIARY
or
INTELLIGENCE SUMMARY. 9th F.A.M.T?

(Erase heading not required.)

Place	Date	Hour	Summary of Events and Information	Remarks and references to Appendices
Gill	1/10/16	—	CONTINUED.	
			63901 Cpl. Witham. J. Clas Wounded in Action Remaining on Duty	
. .	. .	—	38555 Cpl. Scott. A.E. Clas Killed " "	
. .	. .	—	31640 Pr. Innes. J. Clas Wounded " "	
. .	. .	—	9254 Ser. Williamson H. Clas Wounded " " "	
. .	1/10/16	—	115820 Dr. Burns. W. H.Q. Wounded " " Remaining on Duty	

21st Divisional Artillery.

94th BRIGADE R. F. A.

NOVEMBER 1916.

WAR DIARY or INTELLIGENCE SUMMARY

Army Form C. 2118

9th H. Brigade R.F.A.

November 1916

Place	Date	Hour	Summary of Events and Information	Remarks and references to Appendices
NOEULLES	6		Bombardment of T.M. at H7a 2075 carried out by D Bty in accordance with 27th Divl Arty Order BM 231/r	Sheet 36cNW
	7		We flew a new art O/P at G.17.c.85.35 - B & C Batteries husged both sides of their and D Bty. Arllis Street Junction at R.12.a.10.87 and R.12.a.03.72.	
	8	7.15 pm	Bombardment of T.M. at R.S.d.60.43 in accordance with 27th Div Arty Order BM 231/r by 9th	
	15	12.30	Bombardment of Bde. HQy, Front line trench G.S.d.50.16 - R.S.d.9.2 by C and D Btys. 27th DA BM 231/r of 10/11/16	
	18	5.15 pm	Bombardment of enemy trenches and tramway systems round ST ELIE	
	20		In cooperation with Trench Mortars the front and support trenches from G.17.a.9.1 to H.13.a.3.9 were bombarded.	
	24		Bombardment of trenches from G.13.d.48.15 to G.13.d.38.45 (N. 27th DA BM 231/r of 19/11/16)	

Army Form C. 2118.

WAR DIARY
or
INTELLIGENCE SUMMARY. 94th Bde R.F.A

(Erase heading not required.)

November 1916

Place	Date	Hour	Summary of Events and Information	Remarks and references to Appendices
NOEUX LES	2nd		Bombardment of CITÉ ST. ELIE and trenches in G.15.b and d by 1st Corps Heavy artillery, 94th and 95th Bdes. During this bombardment D Bty had premature in bore which killed 1 man and wounded 3 and destroying gun. Capt. A C Mac Q Taylor joined and posted to C. Battery. Casualties	A.2209 OO N° 2 25/11/16
	6th		N° 30844 Gunner Owens R. J. B Bty – killed by falling of portable sound roof.	
	27th		N° 63800 A/Bdr. Williams D.R. killed N° 45901 Sgt Down M. and N°46703 Sa Magstaff of D Bty. " Gassed (wounded)" Sa J Downey " Gassed by premature	
			Honours Awards	
	10th		2/Lt E.G. J Drewer of A.Bty. M.C	
	28th		N° 63890 Cpl I A Gannon A/Bty. M.M.	
			" 76800 " C. McIntern " M.M.	
			" 19686 Dr C.B. Caygill " M.M.	
			" 43800 Sgt. T.H. Roberts D " M.M.	

Bv. Druie Lt Col
Cmdg 94 XBde R.F.A

4th DA

War Diary

for month of November is forwarded.

26/11/16

A P Dunnex Lt
for OC 94th SA Bde

21st Divisional Artillery.

94th BRIGADE R. F. A.

DECEMBER 1916.

WAR DIARY or INTELLIGENCE SUMMARY

Army Form C. 2118.

9th Brigade R.G.A.

Vol / 6

December 1916

Place	Date	Hour	Summary of Events and Information	Remarks and references to Appendices
Various Sectors	11		The fixed shoot of the Enemy Trench Tramway system carried out in conjunction with 21st DA Bh 231/2	Sheet 36 N.W.
	14		Brigade shoot on Enemy trenches and defences north of ST ELOI in H.1.d	
	16		Bombardment of the enemy works at the SALIENT R.12.d.5.8 carried out in accordance with 21st DA 60 N°5	
	20		Bombardment of Enemy defences from H.7.c.0.3 to G.13.d.8.0.6.7 carried out in accordance with 21st DA 60 N°6	
	23		Enemy trench mortars very lively in morning many fires given and Trench Mortars silenced. Divisional Artillery enemy not ascertained, but returned in retaliation Artillery portion in trenches Offran 10 R. Killed 3 O.R. wounded	
	24 to 26		Trench mortar activity not throughout these days & at irregular intervals in shelling Enemy trenches	

WAR DIARY
or
INTELLIGENCE SUMMARY.

Army Form C. 2118.

9th Brigade, R.F.A.

December 1916

Place	Date	Hour	Summary of Events and Information	Remarks and references to Appendices
	1		Casualties	
			N° SE/4944 Sgt Lee A (AVC attached) wounded.	
			„ 36553 Bdr Burke W (9/4) wounded	
			„ 15305 Gr Agnis attached 9/4 from 35th Am S.P. wounded	
	2/3		N° 67994 Gr Carling G (A/9/4) wounded	
	2/4		2/Lt P.H.S Bryandenhurst - 9/9 - & B/O Buttles N° 36881 Bnr Butler S	
			all killed in A Bty	
			N° 76517 Sgt Lawler R.W (A/9/4) wounded	
			N° 136650 Gr Manning A and N° 63606 Gr Thorpe H 4th D/A Bty	
			wounded but returned to duty	
			Honours awards	
	3		N° 10765 Gr Hugglestin of D Bty awarded M.M	

McInnes Capt
for 9.9 R.F.A. Bde

McInnes Capt
for 9.9 R.F.A. Bde

94 th Bde: R.F.A.
Vol: 4

No. 7931

WAR DIARY or INTELLIGENCE SUMMARY

January 1917   **91st Brigade RGA**

Place	Date	Hour	Summary of Events and Information	Remarks and references to Appendices
Merville	3		Two sections of "wreck" A.B.C. Btys and 1 section of D Battery relieved by Batteries of 21st Brigade R.G.A. 6th Div. The relieving sections marching to billets in RAIMBERT	Maps/moves Sheet 36B
	4		Remaining sections of Batteries relieved, and marched to RAIMBERT	
Raimbert	15		6 and D Btys ordered to reinforce the line and marched that night at 10pm and were in action by daybreak on following morning. Batteries came under the orders of 2nd Div Arty	
	19		6 and D Btys returned to training area at RAIMBERT	
	23		Orders for the relief of 21st Div Arty by 21st Div Arty received	21st DA Instruction No. 1
	26		Brigade warned to be ready to march at an Early hour tomorrow	
	27	5.50am	21st DA Operation order No. 11 received	
		9am	Brigade marched to NEUF BERQUIN and went into billets	Hazebrouck 5a.
	28		March continued and billets at WATAU	
	29/31		NATAU	

January 1917 WAR DIARY 94th Brigade RGA
or
INTELLIGENCE SUMMARY.

Place	Date	Hour	Summary of Events and Information	Remarks and references to Appendices
	1		Honours Awards	
			N° 36360 Sgt E.C. Stokes M.G.M Military Medal	
			„ 36943 Bm. F. Loveridge M.G.M Do.	

W Ellynthin
Comdg 94th Brigade RGA

94th Brigade R.F.A.

WAR DIARY
INTELLIGENCE SUMMARY

February 1917

Vol 18

Place	Date	Hour	Summary of Events and Information	Remarks and references to Appendices
Billets at WATOU	1-11			
	12		Brigade marches to HAZEBROUCK	
	13		" " MT BERNENCHON	
	15		Batteries of Brigade relieve batteries of 2nd Brigade RFA 6th Div. Remaining Batteries relieved. Relief completed at 9.20 pm and ammunition places. Batteries in same positions as previously occupied - covering QUARRIES SECTOR.	Sheet 36cNW
	16			
	22		Dummy raid in HOHENZOLLERN Sector. B,C & D Batteries cooperating	

J. Bainton Lt Col
Comdg 94. Bde R.F.A.

9th Brigade RBA
WAR DIARY or INTELLIGENCE SUMMARY
March 1917

Army Form C. 2118.

Place	Date	Hour	Summary of Events and Information	Remarks and references to Appendices
VERMELLES	4		Our sections of each Battery withdrew from the line and marched to BELLERIVE.	
	5		Remaining section withdrew and joined remainder at BELLERIVE. Position remained empty with exception of C Battery which was relieved by C Battery 95th Bde.	
	6		Bde HQ Hrs marched from NOEUX les MINES and joined Batteries at BELLERIVE.	
	11		C Battery moved from BELLERIVE to MT BERNENCHON. Brigade marched to BERGUENEUSE - ANVIN area.	
	13		Brigade marched to BOURBERS-SUR-CANCHE.	
	14		Brigade marched to LUCHEUX.	
	16		O.C. & Bty commanders with working parties of 20 men per battery reported to 149th Bde RBA 30th Div Arty at DAINVILLE and started to prepare positions.	
	23		Sections of Batteries ordered to march to WAILLY - one section taken on the road.	
	26		Brigade marched to ADINFER WOOD and bivouaced.	

Army Form C. 2118.

94th Bde RFA

WAR DIARY
or
INTELLIGENCE SUMMARY

March 1917

Place	Date	Hour	Summary of Events and Information	Remarks and references to Appendices
	29		Batteries went into action near BOISLEUX au MONT Brigade H.Q. was at BOIRY ST. RICTRUDE.	Sheet 51.B S.W.

F.W. Bairstow Col.
Cmdg 94th Bde RFA

9th Div RGA WAR DIARY

April 1917

INTELLIGENCE SUMMARY

Place	Date	Hour	Summary of Events and Information	Remarks and references to Appendices
BOIRY ST RICTRUDE	2	am 5.15	Zero hour. Attacks on the CROISILLES - HENIN Road from T.17.c.70.05 to T.3.d.1.9. in conjunction with 7th Div on our right to attack CROISILLES and 30th Div on left to attack HENIN-sur-COJEUL. The attack made by 13th North. Fusiliers on right (T.17.c.9. to T.10.c.6.) and 15th Northumberland Fusiliers on left (T.10.c.6. to T.3.d.1.9.) The attack supported by artillery as follows:- Rt Group 95th Bde RGA and Rt Art Group, 29th Bde RGA (less A/79) covering 13th North. Fusiliers. and Left Group 94th Bde RGA and Left Sub Group 29th Art RGA (Lt Col Clark) and A/79. covering 15th North Fusiliers. Wyrekos guard as also the villages of CROISILLES by 7th Div and HENIN-sur-COJEUL by 30th Div. 63rd Inf Bde relieved by 64th Inf Brigade on the front T.11.c. out. to T.3.d. 1.9.	Reference Sheet 51B SW. 1/20000 2nd DA. 60 No. 19
	3/4			2nd DA OO: 33 ans 34.
	4/5 (Video)		Bombardment of enemy defences preliminary to general attacks on enemy's main line of Defences commenced. Zones allotted were Right Group from the Sensee River U.9.a.7.5. to T.5.centre to U.2.c.1.6 to N.36.6.5.4. Left Group T.5 centre to HENIN-HENINEL Road N.3.a.4.6. inclusive to N.36.6.5.4 to N.29.a.9.5. - Batteries allotted for wire cutting A/94 and A/79.	

9th K.R.R. WAR DIARY April 1917.
Army Form C. 2118.

or

INTELLIGENCE SUMMARY.

(Erase heading not required.)

Place	Date	Hour	Summary of Events and Information	Remarks and references to Appendices
	6.		M.gun wire shelled suffering no killed and 2 guns damaged (Lewis T8 & 3 3)	Reference Sheets 51.B.S.W.
	7		Gun wire shelled suffering no killed and 2 guns damaged (Lewis T10 a 2.4)	do.
	9		General attacks of enemy's main line of defence. Objectives of 3rd Division. (a) Front line of German trenches T5a.5.2 to HENIN—HENINEL Road	3rd Dp Op. 36
			(b.) 2nd Line from T5a.7.7 to HENIN-HENINEL Road
			(C.) Establish on a line from N30c.0.5.90 to join present line at T10.d.9.1
		4.15 am	Zero. Attack carried out by 1st E.Yorks on right — 1st D.L.I on centre and 9th Royal on left (one 6th & 8th Bns.) supported by artillery as follows:— Left Group (9th Bde + 29th Bde and 2/39 Battery) Creeping barrage on a line T5c.7.9 - N34.d.4.0 - N34c.5.6 - N34a.3.4, lifting at intervals until reaching a line N36a.3.4 + N29b.6.0 - N29.a.2.0
			Summary of Operations. The Right Battalion got through wire and Established front two front line — Centre and Left Battalion did not get through wire.
		6.45	Enemy counter-attacked and drove our infantry (Rt Battalion) out of front line trenches.

94th Bde R.F.A.

Army Form C. 2118.

WAR DIARY April 1917

INTELLIGENCE SUMMARY

3

(Erase heading not required.)

Place	Date	Hour	Summary of Events and Information	Remarks and references to Appendices
	10/10		Line held by our infantry at end of operations – T.5.a.5.3 to N.34.d.5.5 – Minor operations and attacks on Hindenburg Line by 60th Inf. Bde. and 63rd Inf Bde. which failed to gain objectives.	2nd D.A. BO's 37/38
	13.		Attacks arranged to capture first and second line trenches on a front T.5.a.4.5.2 to T.4.b.9.9. Infantry patrols sent out reported that enemy had evacuated his front line trench.	4th D.A. 80 ag
		11.35 a.m.	12 Northumberland Fusiliers on right and 13 K.O.Y.L.I. Infantry on left occupied evacuated german trenches. 58th Divisional Artillery relieved by 37th Divisional Artillery – 290th Bde R.F.A. by 150th Bde and 291st by 151st Bde. – 153rd Bde R.F.A. 133rd Bde R.F.A. relieved left sub group. The line held by 63rd Infantry Brigade that night was T.10.d.5.3 – T.5.a.4.5.2 – N.35.a.8.8. at which point it touched with 56th Division.	
	13.	4.55 p.m.	63rd Inf Bde attacks with objective U.13.b.3.6 – Sunken road U.8.a. and C. – Eastern edge of FONTAINE-lez-CROISILLES – SENSEE River at U.2.b.3.3 – N.E. edge of WOOD in U.2.b. – Bde. not yet by Bde until objective U.13.c.3 – U.13.d.3.6. The attack is held up by machine guns and	2nd D.A. G.O. N°247
		7.50 p.m.	Orders received that Corps had ordered suspension of attacks.	

Army Form C. 2118.

9th Bde HQ RA WAR DIARY April 1917 4

INTELLIGENCE SUMMARY.

(Erase heading not required.)

Place	Date	Hour	Summary of Events and Information	Remarks and references to Appendices
	13		63rd Inf. Brigade relieved by 19th Inf Bde taking over a line from N33 d 3095 thro' N30 c. T5 to T5d T5a and T. on the road.	
	14	5.30am	Attack by VI and VII Corps. Objectives of 37th Div. 1st Line T6b 6.5 - N36 d 6.6 - O31 c 3.6 2nd. Sunken road U7c 0.6 - U1 d 8.9 - U3 a 5.7 The attack made by 19th Inf. Brigade. Objective not gained and the line held at night was N36 a 7.7 to N36 c 5.5 and from T6 a 5.5.6 T6 c 7.5	37th D.A. OO 43.
	15th a.m		Bombardment of enemy defences and approaches in accordance with above.	2nd DA OO2 4th DA 45- 49
	"	7.30 p.	Practice Barrage carried out.	
	23	4.45	Attack by the 33rd Division by the 100th Inf Brigade and 98th Infantry Bde covered by artillery of 21st Div. 150th Army 2nd Artillery Bde and 37th Div 4.H. Objectives. 100th Inf Bde. To capture portion of HINDENBURG Line between 80 Central and SENSEE River. 98th Inf Bde. To gain a line T6 central- Road Junction O31 c and to capture HINDENBURG Line as far as the Sensee River. Infantry failed to gain their objective and passing through varying stages were driven back into their original lines at about 2/pm.	2nd DJ7 OO 49

9th/10th Bn RWF WAR DIARY April 1917

INTELLIGENCE SUMMARY.

Place	Date	Hour	Summary of Events and Information	Remarks and references to Appendices
	23.	6pm	Attack on whole army front renewed with objectives and tasks the same as morning. Attack was again not successful, and an Enemy counter attack we were driven back and occupied a line as previous to morning attack. General bombardment on whole front.	3rd Dn. O.O. A-30
	24/30.		Casualties	2nd Dn. AB's S1. 62/3/4/5.
	7th		2/Lt E.G.S. Dennis M.C. wounded A/94	
	6th		No 13108 Pte. J. Norton Killed	
	3rd		No 36551 Sr. O. Mayo Wounded B/94	
			" 34906 Dr. 2.S. Brown "	
	13th		Lt. P.M.S. Brownlow "	
	30.		No 75527 Sr. A.J. Powe "	
	23		Mjr E.B. Reid "	
	31/3/17			remaining at duty
				do (Remainder)
	4/4/17		N.36140.B.h.R. Ikalyn C/94	
			" 96435 " S. Goddard "	
			" 19.50 Sr. W. Evans "	
			35274 Sr. Burke "	
			" 9.8652 Sr. H. Morris Killed	
			" 102254 Sgt Bon. G.J. Sharpe wounded	
	9/4/17		" 97856 Sr. W. Booker "	remaining at duty

Army Form C. 2118.

9th Bn R.D.F. WAR DIARY April 1917

INTELLIGENCE SUMMARY.

(Erase heading not required.)

Instructions regarding War Diaries and Intelligence Summaries are contained in F.S. Regs., Part II. and the Staff Manual respectively. Title pages will be prepared in manuscript.

Place	Date	Hour	Summary of Events and Information	Remarks and references to Appendices
			Casualties Cents.	
	28/3/17		No. 84077 Pte. W. Jones. D/9th Honours - Remaining at duty	
	31/3/17		" 42588 Sr. P.J. Danton " Died of wounds	
	7/4/17		" 46647 Pte. T. Bere " Wounded.	
	11/4/17		" 46618 A/Pte. W. Plemmer " do	
	13/4/17		" 11487 Sr. McBride " do	
			" 12575 " Marriott " do	
			Honours + Awards	
	3/4/17		No. 82973. Sr. A.S. Blacker. B/9th Military Medal	
			" 55361. Pte. J. Phipps " do	
			" 42875 Sr. R. Whalley M/9th Bar to Military Medal.	
	23/4/17		" 34766 Sr. T.H. Wood " Military Medal.	
			" 46651 " A. Fisher D/9th do	
	30/4/17		" 36003 a/Sr. A. Savage. 9/9th do	
			" 47751 Pte. F. Brown D/9th do	

J. Prinselr
Lieut Col
Comm 9th R D Fus

Army Form C. 2118.

WAR DIARY
or
INTELLIGENCE SUMMARY.

of Gpt94 R.G.A. May 1917

(Erase heading not required.)

Place	Date	Hour	Summary of Events and Information	Remarks and references to Appendices
	29.	1.55a	Zerohour. Attacks by 19th Inf Bde and 98th Inf Bde with objectives 19th Inf Bde - Captures TUNNEL Trench (HINDENBURG Supports) between plum lane and CROISILLES - FONTAINE Road. 98th Inf Bde - TUNNEL Trench between SENSÉE River and CROISILLES - FONTAINE Road. The attack by 19th Inf Bde failed, the infantry not reaching their objectives and were reported back in their original line at 2.14 pm The attack by 98th Inf Bde captures HINDENBURG Support as far as hamp lane. C Battery withdrawn from action to Rest Camp. 2nd Div. (Infantry) relieved 33rd Div Infantry	33rd DA GO N° 4
	29 31/1??	4	Casualties. N° 63687 Gr. E. Mentz. A/94 died of wounds 11/5/17 . 86278 Bdr. B.J. Vickery " sheet chock 30/5/17 . 87963 Gr. W.H. Brecton B/94 wounded (at duty) 11/5/17	

Army Form C. 2118.

9th Bde R.F.A. May 1917 2nd

WAR DIARY or INTELLIGENCE SUMMARY

9th Bde. R.H.A. Vol 21

Place	Date May	Hour	Summary of Events and Information	Remarks and references to Appendices
BOIRY	2		Bde Headquarters moved to Sunken road T10 c 0.8.	Sheet 51B SW 1/20000
BEGUGNE	3	3.45 am	General attack along the front. 18th Div on our right attacked by 62nd and 110th Infantry Brigades with objectives (a) Blue Line: The line of Sensée River. (b) Yellow Line T18 b.5.3 – U7c.0.0 – U7c.5.5 – U7d.1.5 – U7d.7.7 – U8c.0.8 U8a.5.4 – U8b.0.7 – U2a.4.0 – U2d.6.4. 62nd Inf Bde Objective: Blue and Yellow Line Sn. of HINDENBURG Front Trench (exclusive) 62nd Inf Bde Objective: HINDENBURG Front and Support Trenches b. Army Boundary U14 a 20 – U14 a 5.3. 110th Inf Bde Objective: Blue & Yellow Line NE of HINDENBURG Support Trench (exclusive) Liaison with 110th Inf Bde. The attack was not successful and the line hes at end of May was approximately. HINDENBURG Front line on for as Vic40 and Support Line to U10 c 5 by 62nd Inf Bde – 110th Inf Bde trenches rue from V10 c 3	2nd Div to 57

Army Form C. 2118.

-2-

9th Bde RGA WAR DIARY May 1917
or INTELLIGENCE SUMMARY

(Erase heading not required.)

Place	Date	Hour	Summary of Events and Information	Remarks and references to Appendices
	4/5		& Cross Roads V.1.d.5-9 & Wood Trench about V.2.a.1.5 - 62nd Inf Bde in the morning. Infantry which no patrols 62nd Inf Bde (less 10th yorks) took over from 110th Inf Bde defences N.E. of Hindenburg Line - 110th Inf Bde took 10th Yorks defences S.W. of Hindenburg Line - 62nd Inf Bde continue to hold Hindenburg Line. Liaison with 62nd Inf Bde.	
	10		D. Battery withdraws to wagon lines for a rest.	
	10th		Relief of 2nd Division (less Artillery) by 33rd Division	
	12th		2nd Div Arty relieved by 37th Div Arty (Brig Gen F Potts CMG).	Cherisy
	14		D Battery moves into position again	Vraux
	20	5:15am	Zero hour. Attack by 19th Inf Bde - 100th Inf Bde and 98th Inf Bde with objective HINDENBURG LINE	37th Div
			100th Inf Bde. the line between the CROISILLES - HENDECOURT and CROISILLES	00.57
			- FONTAINE Road	
			98th Inf Bde. to attack S.E. down the HINDENBURG LINE from present North as far as the CROISILLES - FONTAINE Road	

Army Form C. 2118.

WAR DIARY
or
INTELLIGENCE SUMMARY.

(Erase heading not required.)

Opp. Bn. RDF   May 1917

Place	Date	Hour	Summary of Events and Information	Remarks and references to Appendices

19th Inf Bde - attack the HUMP in U14c and form defensive flank from U14c 1.3 to area north at U14 c 5.9 to Inf Bde - R. Battalion.

The attack both successful and the front line of the HINDENBURG line was captured and held by 100th Inf Bde, but fewer Essigaline Support line.

The attack by 95th Inf Bde reached a point about 30 yds North of River Road in the Supports and gained touch with the 100th Inf Bde at the FONTAINE-CROISILLES Road.

7.30 p.m. Zero hour for second attack with further HINDENBURG Supports. Attack being carried out by 19th Inf Bn with objective that part of line between NEURY LANE and FONTAINE CROISILLES Rd. The 95th Inf Bde continuing attack down HINDENBURG Support - 19th Inf Bde did not reach objective and remained shell holes about 150 x this side.

The 95th Inf Bde were more successful and advanced to a point 60 yds north of the SENSÉE Riv.

Army Form C. 2118.

WAR DIARY
or
INTELLIGENCE SUMMARY.

(Erase heading not required.)

5 / Gp. N.Dn. R.S.A.   May 1917

Place	Date	Hour	Summary of Events and Information	Remarks and references to Appendices

Casualties

Ors.

N° 63565. Dr. W. Kenny - Killed 1/5/17 C/94
" 31290. Dr. W.H. Evans - Wounded 11/5/17 C/94   } began line shelter. Bony Bezauco Eawin
" 48290. Sgt. H.J. Jeffries - Wounded 18/5/17 C/94 (remaining at duty)
" 21 Lt. E.W.C. Amott - Wounded 7/9/17 -
N° 36276. Br. F. Massey - Wounded 24/5/17
" 79434. " S. Kendrick - Wounded 24/5/17 (remaining at duty)
" 51584. ASM. W.H. Pentrys - Wounded 28/5/17 D/94 (at duty)

Honours & Awards

N° 34766. Sr. T.H. Wood - Military Medal 1/5/17 M/94
" 36181. Gpon. T. Return -   "   24/5/17 "
" 63687. Sr. B. Meads - Bar to do   24/5/17 "
" 36603. Gpon R. Savage - Military Medal 1/5/17 C/94
" 49751. Ror. Fr. D. Prowse " do   1/5/17 D/94
" 46651. Sr. C. Breton   " do   1/5/17 D/94

Copy 91st Bue R.S.A. line

2.

WAR DIARY or INTELLIGENCE SUMMARY

9th Bde R.F.A.   June 1917

Army Form C. 2118.

Place	Date	Hour	Summary of Events and Information	Remarks and references to Appendices
	19/20 24/26		Retal(?) 1. 21st Div (less Artillery) by 33rd Div (plus Artillery) Bombardment of enemy defences by Corps trenches and Divl Artillery	21st DA OO No 73 22nd DA HO 74 38th DA OO No 9
	23/24	Midnight	Attack by 19th Inf Bde on TUNNEL TRENCH with objective TUNNEL TRENCH from LUMP LANE (U9.L.4.4) and to form flank in TUNNEL TRENCH at U9.L.6.0. The attack was not successful	
	26	12.30am	Attack by 50th Div on a line U16.5.0 - U.1.4.9.7 - 95th Bde RFA co-operated, but not this Brigade. The attack was unsuccessful and prisoners taken. A Battery and 1 section D. Battery withdrawn from line for Rest.	38th DA OO No 13
	29	6.30am	Attack by 100th Inf Bde on DUNNE TRENCH, south of CROISILLES FONTAINE Road. The attack was not successful.	33rd DA O6 No 15

Army Form C. 2118.

6th Bde R.F.A. June 1917

WAR DIARY or INTELLIGENCE SUMMARY

Place	Date	Hour	Summary of Events and Information	Remarks and references to Appendices
Hd Truppn St LEGER	1		Infantry of 33rd Div relieved by Infantry 21st Div. 100th Inf Bde by 62nd Inf Bde in Right Sector – Covered by 94th Bde RFA. 98 do by 64th Inf Bde in Left Sector. 19 do by 110th Inf Bde in Reserve.	1/100000 Sheet 51 BSW
	8	11.30 pm	58th Division on our right carried out raid on front HINDENBURG LINE between U20.a.8.9 and U20.h.1545. 2nd Div Arty assisted in forming barrage. The raid was successful and 'prisoners taken.	2nd D.A. OO. 67
	14		Col JM Bannatine CMG relinquished command of the Brigade and proceeded to England. Major D Paris MC assumed temporary command of Brigade	
	15	2.50 am	Attack by 58th Div on HINDENBURG front line U20.h.4.2 & U14.c.3.9 2nd Div Arty assisted by forming Chinese barrage. The attack was successful	2nd D.A. OO 11/270
	16	3.10 am	Attack by 21st Div and 58th on TUNNEL TRENCH - Objective of 21st Div from U14.c.40.5 to junction of LUMP LANE and TUNNEL TRENCH. The attack was unsuccessful not successful.	2nd D.A. OO 69

Army Form C. 2118.

4th Bde CMA WAR DIARY June 1917
or INTELLIGENCE SUMMARY.
(Erase heading not required.)

Instructions regarding War Diaries and Intelligence Summaries are contained in F. S. Regs., Part II. and the Staff Manual respectively. Title pages will be prepared in manuscript.

Place	Date	Hour	Summary of Events and Information	Remarks and references to Appendices
			Casualties	
			2/Lt. L. Lauchlan – 2nd T.M. Bde attached B/94. 4/6/17 wounded – Remaining at Duty.	
			No. 1715. Dr. P. Braidy B/94 do do	
			No. 79948. Cpl. C. Bowden D/94 5/6/17 Killed	
			" 876010 Sr. E. Yallop " " Wounded	
			65789 " J. Sergeant " " do (Shell Shock)	
			876187 " H.R. Legon " 17/6/17 do	
			55479 " R.C. Dancy " 27/6/17 do	
			5304 7 " C.T. Clayton " do do	
			876169 Bdr. T. Misson " 23/6/17 do (Remaining at Duty)	
			87619 Gr. Lt. Dean " do do	
			140731 " J.E.M. Todd " do do	
			Honours & Awards	
			Lieut. H. Dane. Awarded M.C. 37th Dn. R.O. 1/6/17	
			Major W. T. Lyimmett. D.S.O. do 9/6/17 (late army 9/94)	
			A/Major G.E.W. Franklyn. Brevet Majority. do 9/6/17	

Army Form C. 2118.

4 / A.H.Bde. R.G.A. WAR DIARY or INTELLIGENCE SUMMARY.

June 1917.

(Erase heading not required.)

Place	Date	Hour	Summary of Events and Information	Remarks and references to Appendices
			The following mentioned in dispatches of 9/4/17 intr Aug 9/4. Major W. J. Synnott E.F.W. Franklyn M.C. a/Capt H.W. Collins a/Capt D.S. Tarbyrn Lieut M. Turner.	

Blair Major R.A.
Comg 4 A.Brigade R.G.A.

Army Form C. 2118.

Ork. Bde RGA.   July 1917

Vol 23

WAR DIARY
INTELLIGENCE SUMMARY.

(Erase heading not required.)

Instructions regarding War Diaries and Intelligence Summaries are contained in F. S. Regs., Part II. and the Staff Manual respectively. Title pages will be prepared in manuscript.

Place	Date	Hour	Summary of Events and Information	Remarks and references to Appendices
HQ Tro H.Q. 4 Shot SP S of	2		2/Lieut H.A. Boys D.S.O. joined from 3rd Canadian Divsion and assumed command of the Brigade.	
	7		A Battery returned to the line from being at rest in wagon lines. D Battery withdrawn from the line to Rest Camp at HENDECOURT, guns remaining in action and being manned by detachment of 93rd Bde R.G.A.	Shut Sp Sg Vagoon
	8		1st Lot Bde relieved by 110th Infantry Brigade in the Right Sector. Incl[uding] from VIS en O.1 to the SENSEE RIVER at Vy 9 1574. 7th Leic Regt relieving 9th KOYLI — Right Subsector — 6th Leic relieving 10th KOYLI in Left Sub sector — 5th Leic Regt relieving 15th Durham L.I. in Support, and 9th Leic. Regt. relieving 1st E Yorks R. in Reserve.	
	14		D. Battery returned to the line from Rest Camp. 1 new Battalion Relief — 6th Leic Regt relieving 6th Leic Regt — 9th Leic Regt relieving 7th Leic Regt.	
	20		1 new Battalion Relief — 6th Leic Regt relieving 6th Leic Regt — 9th Leic Regt relieving 8th Leic Regt — 7th Leic Regt relieving 9th Leic Regt.	

Army Form C. 2118.

WAR DIARY
or
INTELLIGENCE SUMMARY.
(Erase heading not required.)

9th Bde R.G.A. July 1917

Instructions regarding War Diaries and Intelligence Summaries are contained in F.S. Regs., Part II. and the Staff Manual respectively. Title pages will be prepared in manuscript.

Place	Date	Hour	Summary of Events and Information	Remarks and references to Appendices
	24/25	midnight	Raid by 6th Ino Regt took place — Raiding party known on the alert and returned	Sheet S1.9 S.W
	25	2.50am	Raid by 7th Ino Regt took place "MEBU" at U14 a 1.9" — Raiding party found that wire remained an obstacle and returned. Wire was cutting for time raids had been carried out by Trench mortars.	110th Inf Bde O.O.99
			Co-operative programme of fire by 15th Batteries was arranged to cover the withdrawal of the Raiding party which was only partially carried out, mid being received that all the parts were back in our trenches.	9th Bde O.O. N°47
	26		Inter Battalion Relief; 9th Ino Regt. relieving 7 Ino Regt - 8th Ino Regt relieving 6th Ino Regt	
	10		N° 32616. Sgt. R. Taylor A. Bty wounded	
			Casualties	
			Honours & Awards	
	17		Lieut C.S. Frost D Bty awarded Military Cross	

[signature]
Comdg 9th Bde R.G.A. Coz.

29th Bde R.G.A. War Diary or Intelligence Summary

August 1917 — Vol 24

Army Form C. 2118.

Place	Date	Hour	Summary of Events and Information	Remarks and references to Appendices
H.Qrs. Trot 7.4 Ghel. 51.b.S.W.	1		68th Infantry Brigade relieved by 110th Infantry Brigade in Tunnel Sector	
	9		62nd Infantry Brigade relieved by 110th Infantry Brigade in Left Sector	
	13		Brigade Headquarters moved from Trot 7.4 to Esh Infantry Brigade Headquarters at Trot 4.0	
	15	10.45pm	Raid by 1st & 6th Yorks Regiment with objective of gaining identification. Raiding party found that wire was intact and returned. A Co-operative programme of fire by 18pr. Batteries was arranged to cover withdrawal of raiding party which was only partially carried out, wire being reserved that the party had returned.	
	18		110th Infantry Brigade relieved by 62nd Infantry Brigade in Left Sector	
	25		Orders received in connection of relief of 21st Division by 16th Division	
			110th Infantry Brigade relieved by 49th Infantry Brigade in Reserve	
	26		68th Infantry Brigade relieved by 49th Infantry Brigade in Right Sector	
	27		62nd Infantry Brigade relieved by 48th Infantry Brigade in Left Sector	
	30/31		Batteries A B & D Batteries relieved by sections of 180th Brigade R.G.A. Batteries	29th DAO.81

Army Form C. 2118.

4th Bde RFA

WAR DIARY
or
INTELLIGENCE SUMMARY.

August 1917

(Erase heading not required.)

Instructions regarding War Diaries and Intelligence Summaries are contained in F. S. Regs., Part II. and the Staff Manual respectively. Title pages will be prepared in manuscript.

Place	Date	Hour	Summary of Events and Information	Remarks and references to Appendices
	31/8		Remainder of A B & D Batteries withdrawn and the whole of C Battery, the Index position not being occupied – all batteries and Brigade quarters withdrawing to wagon lines at Boisseux – au – Mont.	4th DA OO N° 98 and 3/2 DA OO N° 87

J. P. Ommundsen Capt RFA.
for OC 4th Bde RFA.

WAR DIARY or INTELLIGENCE SUMMARY

92nd Brigade RFA

September 1917

Army Form C. 2118.

Place	Date	Hour	Summary of Events and Information	Remarks and references to Appendices
	1/5 6/7		Headquarters and all Batteries at wagon lines BOISLEUX-AU-MONT. Brigade entrained at ARRAS detraining at CAESTRE marched to FLETRE and billeted.	Sheep Farm HAZEBROUCK 6A
	11		Working parties sent up to prepare battery positions.	
	17		Sections of Batteries marched to RENINGHELST going into action that night relieving batteries of 106th Brigade RFA, 2nd Division.	
	13		Headquarters & remaining sections of Batteries marched to RENINGHELST occupying wagon lines of 106th Bde RFA - relief of 106th Batteries completed that night. H.Q.C. Bty's grouped with A Group Col Cadan 190th Bde RFA D Bty grouped with Col Symond Group H.Q. Divisional Artillery under command of H.Q. Divisional Artillery. Brigade Headquarters did not go into action.	
	20	5.40 am	Zero hour of attack. 2nd Division Artillery under orders of H.Q. D.A. attack by 124th Infantry Brigade on right and 122nd Infantry Brigade on left - 39th Division on right of 41st Div and 23rd Division on left. Successful from all round rich, all objectives were gained.	

Army Form C. 2118.

Place 9th KBde RFA

WAR DIARY
or
INTELLIGENCE SUMMARY. September 1917

2

Date	Hour	Summary of Events and Information	Remarks and references to Appendices
23rd		Batteries came under the orders of 39th Divisional Artillery grouped with 190th Bde RFA and commanded by Lt Col 114 Bde DSO	
26.	6.30 am	Attack by 39th Division with objective 100 yards beyond 101st Trench attack carried out by 118th Infy Bde on the right and by 116th Infy Bde on the left	Sheet ZILLEBEKE Ypres.
29/30		Preparation of new positions near STIRLING CASTLE of new positions of Batteries	

Ian Lloyd
Lt Col.
Cmdg 9th Bde RFA

Army Form C. 2118.

WAR DIARY
or
INTELLIGENCE SUMMARY.

9th AA Brigade R.F.A.   September 1917

(Erase heading not required.)

Place	Date	Hour	Summary of Events and Information	Remarks and references to Appendices
			Casualties	
	26/9/17		Major. D. Paige. wounded. C/9v.	
	26/9/17		2/Lt. W. Rice. Died of wounds. B/9v.	
	26/9/17		Lt. O. Fraser. Lyon. wounds. B/9v.	
	12/9/17		703536 M Bdr. Bury Cross. Q.E. wounded (Sev.) B/9v.	
	12/9/17		816196 Gunner Bongham. L.B. do do	
	12/9/17		" Budham. A.J. do do	
	12/9/17		33624 " Claise. J.J. do do	
	12/9/17		63216 " Logus. J. do do	
	12/9/17		80048 " Saunders. R.A. do do	
	12/9/17		122332 " Wells. W.L.R. do do	
	12/9/17		63749 " Wilson. do do	
	14/9/17		81/6151 " Butterfield. A.J. wounded 6/9v.	
	12/9/17		82434 " Fleetwood. L. do do	
	12/9/17		39765 Driver Anida. W.J. wounded(Gas.) 20.	
	13/9/17		26035 Gunner Wilson. G. wounded A/9v.	
	14/9/17		47178 " Kennett. J.B. wounded A/9v.	
	15/9/17		65527 " Henman. E.B. wounded B/9v.	
	16/9/17		816050 Sgt. Whiting. C. wounded B/9v.	
	17/9/17		3705B Sgt. Costello. A. wounded B/9v.	
	17/9/17		35801 Gunner Thompson. A.J. killed B/9v.	
	17/9/17		19753 " MacFarlane. J. wounded B/9v.	
	8/9/17		129785 Gunner Sadler. H. wounded A/9v.	
	10/9/17		160139 " Ballinta. G.A. wounded 17/9v.	
	17/9/17		27103 " Kennett. J.A. wounded A/9v. remaining at duty.	
	19/9/17		92404 Bdr. Petman. D. wounded C/9v.	
	20/9/17		36181 Bdr. Royle. wounded. B/9v.	
	20/9/17		36890 Gunner Post. a.S. killed B/9v.	
	20/9/17		15529 " wounded B/9v.	

WAR DIARY / INTELLIGENCE SUMMARY

Army Form C. 2118.

Arkhangel 1917

Place	Date	Hour	Summary of Events and Information	Remarks and references to Appendices

Casualties

Date	No.	Rank	Name	Wounded / Killed / Injured	Remarks
20/9/17	760930383	Gunner	Wood J.	Accidentally Injured	2/9/17
20/9/17	88/97	Gunner	Russell O.	Killed	1/9/17
21/9/17	1104	Dr.	Brown B.	Killed	2/9/17
21/9/17	306/5	Gunner	Christopher J.	Killed	2/9/17
22/9/17	801	Gunner	Roberts	Killed	A/94
22/9/17	83/97	Gunner	Rawlins J.	Wounded	4/94
22/9/17	88/32	Gunner	Robins A.	Wounded	5/94
22/9/17	1826	2/Bdr	Ainsworth G.	Wounded	A/94
23/9/17	13850	Sgt	Greenwill W.S.	Wounded	A/94
23/9/17	8/94	Gunner	Sayer H.A.	Wounded	M/94
24/9/17	34/511	Gunner	Davis G.J.	Wounded (Gas)	B/94
24/9/17	70629	Gunner	Ballantine J.	Wounded	B/94
24/9/17	8/691	Bdr	Everscape E.	Wounded	B/94
24/9/17	36923	Driver	Hips L.	Killed	B/94
25/9/17	57530	Sgt	Clarke R.O.	Accidentally Injured	A/94
26/9/17	60360	Gunner	Fairbrother W.	Wounded	B/94 — remaining at duty
26/9/17	15117	Gunner	Manning A.J.	Wounded	C/94 — remaining at duty
26/9/17	13294	Gunner	Jones E.A.	Wounded	D/94 — remaining at duty
26/9/17	86897	Gunner	Thomas G.	Killed	C/94
26/9/17	38670	Bdr	Christie W.	Killed	C/94
26/9/17	07631	Gunner	Bryan J.	Wounded	D/94
26/9/17	55599	Gunner	Bolton J.	Killed	A/94
27/9/17	37605	Gunner	Brass R.J.	Wounded	A/94 Shell Shock
27/9/17	16034	Gunner	Read S.	Wounded	A/94
28/9/17	45629	Sgt	Prescott B.	Killed	A/94
30/9/17	83/07	Gunner	Ruston J.H.	Wounded	M/94
30/9/17	62665	Gunner	Legan L.	Wounded (Gas)	12/94
30/9/17	8/34	Gunner	Thomas a.	Wounded	13/94
30/9/17	13630	Driver	Hunt J. H.	Wounded	B/94
30/9/17	76138	Driver	Peter W.J.	Wounded	B/94 — remaining at duty
30/9/17	30870	Driver	Walkers J.	Wounded	

Army Form C. 2118.

WAR DIARY
or
INTELLIGENCE SUMMARY

(Erase heading not required.)

Instructions regarding War Diaries and Intelligence Summaries are contained in F.S. Regs., Part II. and the Staff Manual respectively. Title pages will be prepared in manuscript.

September 1917

Place	Date	Hour	Summary of Events and Information	Remarks and references to Appendices
			Casualties	
	25/9/17		136515 Stratton. R. wounded	1.0.9.04
	26/9/17		259813 Rower wounded	1.9/9.04 3 Signals M.T. Res
	27/9/17		265045 Rainer wounded	27/9/04
	28/9/17		R.O. 31977 Many Sis wounded	1.6/9.04
	29/9/17		27457 Emmer Grindlaye. J. wounded	5/9.04
	29/9/17		371164 Driver Janes. S. wounded	6/9.04
	30/9/17		83448 Driver Wilkinson. R. wounded	6/9.04
	30/9/17		110313 Driver Nelson. H. wounded	6/9.04
	30/9/17		1185.05 Gunner Davies. J. wounded	5/9.04
	30/9/17		46694 Gunner Watson. S.J. wounded	5/9.04
	29/9/17		55405 Driver Connolly. R.S. wounded	07.94
	30/9/17		42900 Driver Thompson. G. wounded	07.94 Shell fire
	30/9/17		155336 Driver Dawson. S. wounded	6/9.04 in ordy.

Hartzigh
Lt. Col.
Comdy 92nd Bde R.F.A.

WAR DIARY or **INTELLIGENCE SUMMARY**

Army Form C. 2118.

9th Bde R.F.A.

Place	Date	Hour	Summary of Events and Information	Remarks and references to Appendices
DORMY HOUSE T.3.a.5.5	1st & 2nd		Completion and occupation of Bty position at STIRLING CASTLE and SANCTUARY WOOD. Registration was also carried out. Battery occupies DORMY HOUSE and became Right Group. Commanded by Lt Colonel M.A. Boyd D.S.O. and consists of A & B/9th 9th B.R.F.A and 11th D/95 Bde R.F.A.	Sheet No.28 N.W. 1/40,000
	3rd	6am	Corps Barrage	
	3rd	3pm	Army Barrage	
	4th	6am	2nd Division attacks with 5 thrown on right, 7th on left. OBJECTIVE:- Line J.11.a.5.5 — J.11.a.65.95 — J.11.d.95.15 — J.12.a.1.55. Right Group Supports by 4 shrapnel & 2 shrapnel barrages.	1:10,000 WESTHOEK
	5	9am	Reorganization of Arty Groups: Right Group commanded by Colonel K.A. Boyd D.S.O. consists of the four Btys of the 9th Bde R.F.A.	
	7th	4.40am	Corps Barrage	
		5.30pm		
	8	5am	Barrage 2nd R.F.A. became Sub-Group under 7 K.D.Group.	
		4.15am	2nd Division withdraws from the line and was relieved by 7th Div. autumn relieves by same on 8 & 8 Oct 1917.	
	9	5.20am	"A" Group (9th Bde R.F.A.) Supports by 7th Div attacks on REUTEL —	

WAR DIARY or INTELLIGENCE SUMMARY

Army Form C. 2118.

9th Brigade R.F.A.

OCTOBER 1917

Place	Date	Hour	Summary of Events and Information	Remarks and references to Appendices
DANNY HOUSE	10th	11:30 am	JUDGE COPSE. JUDGECOTT. ANZACS on our right & I. ANZACS on our left. 7th Division & 5th Division attacked on our right & I. ANZAC Corps advanced most of their objectives. Corps Barrage.	
	11th	6 am	Army Barrage. Incidents of B/94 withdraws to their wagon line their remaining fire manned by A/94.	
	12th	5.10 pm 6.15 am	Corps Barrage. Arty Barrage. 2nd ANZAC Corps attacked PASSCHENDAELE. 7th Div'l Arty Group captured by forming a barrage in depth with a view to stimulating an attack on BECELAERE. 10 am Reorganisation of Arty Group. A Command by Lt Colonel HARVEY DSO. consists of 94 Bde RFA and 15th? 315 Army Bde RFA. Guning 7th Bde 23rd Division and came under the command of Rifle Brigade General Stanley Clarke. C.M.G., D.S.O. Army Barrage.	
	13 L			
	14th	5.15 pm	Personnel of B/94 returned to the line and took over guns manned by A/94. Personnel of A/94 withdrew to their wagon line.	

Army Form C. 2118.

A.H.Q. BM.RJA.

WAR DIARY
or
INTELLIGENCE SUMMARY.

OCTOBER 1917

Place	Date	Hour	Summary of Events and Information	Remarks and references to Appendices
DORMY HOUSE	19		Lt. Col. A. BM. R.J.A. returned to their bound line Colonel JA Higginson D.S.O. resumed command of J.Group and took over Lt Col Sirs. at DORMY HOUSE.	
	20		Re distribution of Army Groups H. Divs. Re BM.R.J.A. returned to the line. Colonel H.A. Boys D.S.O. resumed command of J.Group which consists of 4 gps one R.F.A.	
	26	5.40am	J.Group attacked GHELUVELT and 9th R. Div POLDERHOEK CHATEAU and 10th R.Group carried on a task allotted to it by C.R.A. 5th SA under whose areas it came from zero to zero plus 16x namely searching square J.I.9.a. and for this purpose A/113 Army Bde R.F.A. came under the command of J.Group from zero to zero + 152. J.Group then switched to its defensive line and came under the command of 91st S.A. Brig. General Newcombe D.S.O. 5 Div took POLDERHOEK CHATEAU but lost it again at night.	

Army Form C. 2118.

WAR DIARY
or
INTELLIGENCE SUMMARY

(Erase heading not required.)

Army: 2nd ARMY
Month: OCTOBER 1917

Place	Date	Hour	Summary of Events and Information	Remarks and references to Appendices
ARMY HQrs	29	7.0 pm	7.0 pm returned to the line at POPERINGHE from 2.30 pm.	
	28		Ath Group the Australian Heavy Group under Command Lt Col Harpy DSO. Consists of the 253rd Siege Battery A.S.R.A., 36th Aus. R.F.A., 35th Div. 30th NY House Bys RFA from our position occupied by 8/Sr Army Field Arty.	
	29	5.0 am	Army Barrage	
	30	5.0 am	Army Barrage on the advance on PASSCHENDAELE	
			A Group consist of Siege Batteries fired on the back of the X Corps which was to develop an attack on BROODSEINDE BEZELAERE.	
	31	5.15 am	Corps Barrage	
			Barrages in addition to their actual on operation were frequently carried out on areas noted by aeroplanes and in a few occasions during the two months there has been a barrage fired half an hour between two barrages each day.	
			The position at STIRLING CASTLES were continuously and heavily shelled by the enemy during the month and a great many casualties were caused to detachments. Apparently during practised barrages which were really replied to by shelling this area. There were approximately nine 18pdr batteries in this immediate nearest area belong to R.F.A. 9th AIF 13pdr Bn guns. The casualties to guns were extra ordinary that by the 19th inst our howitzers were manned by the evening from the personnel of batteries of the Bttn. remaining ill (by the end of the month the remaining guns (3 in number)	

Army Form C. 2118.

WAR DIARY
or
INTELLIGENCE SUMMARY.

A Bn RM

OCTOBER 1917

Place	Date	Hour	Summary of Events and Information	Remarks and references to Appendices
Army			Our engineers attempted to put new earthwork forward. The blowing up of the required amount of ammunition was attempted but did not sufficiently and a fair amount during the early part of the month, but owing to the large number of guns put out of action, [illegible] the ammunition dumps were available for the remainder, it was a [illegible] found necessary to attack ammunition later on	

(sd) [signature] B Colonel
Commdg. A Brigade RMA

Army Form C. 2118.

WAR DIARY or INTELLIGENCE SUMMARY.

9th A Brigade R.F.A. Honors + Awards.

October 1917

(Erase heading not required.)

Place	Date	Hour Btty	No. Rank & Name	Summary of Events and Information	Remarks and references to Appendices
In the Field.	6.10.17	B/94	Mr/Bdr Swan H.	Awarded Bar to Military Medal	
	15.10.17	A/94	37206 Cpl Udo R.J.	Awarded Military Medal	
	15.10.17	B/94	18838 Dr. Manship G.	" " "	
	18.10.17	B/94	35089 Gnr Ward T.	" " "	
	18.10.17	H.Q.	259813 Pnr Rugless J.	" " "	
	24.10.17	C	Capt R.H.A.S. Geddes	" Military Cross	
	24.10.17	B	2/Lieut J. Marshall	" " "	
	24.10.17	A	36360 Sgt Stoker E.C.	" Distinguished Conduct Medal	
	24.10.17	A	45400 Cpl Metcalfe A.V.	" Military Medal	
	24.10.17	A	36795 Sgt Mack B.	" " "	
	24.10.17	A	47654 2/Lt Mobbs T.	" " "	
	24.10.17	A	37036 Bdr Newman R.	" " "	
	29.10.17	A	Major R.J. Weir	" Military Cross	
	29.10.17	A	2/Lieut C. Norman	" " "	
	29.10.17	D	39347 Gnr Gilband S.	" Military Medal	

Army Form C. 2118.

WAR DIARY
or
INTELLIGENCE SUMMARY.
(Erase heading not required.)

9th Brigade R.F.A.

CASUALTIES Officers OCTOBER 1917

Place	Date	Hour	Rank	Name	Summary of Events and Information	Remarks and references to Appendices
In the field	2/10/17	9/9A	Captain	E.E. Miller	Wounded.	
	do	do	2/Lieut	E.M. Pearce	Wounded on duty.	
	7/10/17	9/9A	Lieut	J. Scott	Wounded.	
	9/10/17	B18.1	Lieut	B.D. Campbell	Wounded since died of wounds.	
	14/10/17	B/9A	Lieut	R.15.1 Frost	Killed	
	17/10/17	31/9A	Captain	D.S. Failyour	Wounded (Gas) returned to unit after 4 days in hospital	
	do	do	2/Lt	Birrell	Wounded (Gas) do do	
	do	do	2/Lt	R.P. Reid	Wounded (Gas)	
	18/10/17	B/9A	2/Lt	Townsend	Wounded (Gas) as duty	
	19/10/17	5/9A	2/Lt	J.L. Hewitt	Wounded (Gas)	
	20/10/17	9/9A	Major	N.J. Boldade	Wounded (Gas).	
	do	do	2/Lt	G.E. McFarlane	Wounded (Gas).	
	do	do	2/Lt	J.R. Bennett	Wounded (Gas)	
	do	27/9A	2/Lt	J.E. Harding	Killed.	

WAR DIARY
or
INTELLIGENCE SUMMARY.

Army Form C. 2118.

O.C. = Bde R.A.

CASUALTIES ORS. OCTOBER 1917.

Place	Date	Hour	No.	Rank	Name	Summary of Events and Information nature	Remarks and references to Appendices
In the	19/3/17	9.20	21650	Gr	Hutchens P	wounded	
	20	5.30	3736l	Bdr	Nixon R	wounded	
Field	21/6/17	2.30	65824	Sgt	Yarrow JA	wounded	
	22	8.30	143300	Sgt	Hopkins L	wounded	
	22	do	63160	Sgt	Yates A	wounded	
	22	C.Day	132578	Gr	Green H	wounded	
	22	am	27500	Gr	Waddie E	wounded	
	20	do	63805	Gr	Cocke J	wounded	
	22	8.30	129172	Gr	Ward B	wounded	
	31/4/17	4.15	46247	Gr	Harding G	killed	
	20	do	352120	Sgt	Sproe JH	wounded (legs)	
			301013	Cpl	Gormley J	do do	
	20	2.15	30865	Gr	Thurston G	do do	
			125373	Gr	Gent A	do do	
			136190	Gr	Stewart JE	do 26	
			179645	Gr	Wilson A	do no attacks T.M. Bee	
	11/11/17	10/1a	5825	Gr	Keenan J	killed no do	
		A/9/4	255143 261103	R.S.M	Elbert Birch JE	killed	

Army Form C. 2118.

WAR DIARY
or
INTELLIGENCE SUMMARY

(Erase heading not required.)

Army Form C. 2118.

Place	Date	Hour	No.	Rank	Name	Summary of Events and Information	Remarks and references to Appendices
In the Field	2/10/17		34785	Pte	Skaggs H.G.	wounded	
			8956	Pte	Aspden B.	wounded	
			365	Sgt	Gurman ?	killed	
			19449	Sgt	Williams S.J.	killed	
			110577	Sgt	Porter J.	killed	
			15983?	Pte	Tisle R.	wounded	
			22685	Pte	Sorcliffe E.	wounded	
			26847	Pte	Bunce M.C.	killed	
	4/10/17	8/10	53081	Pte	Langford D.	wounded	
			275599	Pte	Mortimer J.	killed	
			2334	Sgt	Preston J.	wounded	attacked from 2M Pola
			17505	Pte	Clegg J.D.	killed	
			76398	Pte	Gilchrist J.	wounded	
			236865	Pte	Kelly B.	wounded	
			23684	Pte	Lockhart H.	wounded	
			30505	Pte	Cummings A.J.	wounded	
			34631	Pte	Hull J.	wounded	
			34075	Pte	Walker J.	wounded	

Army Form C. 2118.

O.W. Bou R.T.A

WAR DIARY
or
INTELLIGENCE SUMMARY.
(Erase heading not required.)

CASUALTIES   OCTOBER 1917.

Instructions regarding War Diaries and Intelligence Summaries are contained in F. S. Regs., Part II. and the Staff Manual respectively. Title pages will be prepared in manuscript.

Place	Date	Hour	No	Rk	Summary of Events and Information	Remarks and references to Appendices
In the Field	4/10/17	13th	102764	Pte	Howe S.J. — killed	
			97707	Pte	Sharp S.J. — wounded.	
		(2)	113245	Pte	Hunts R. — wounded.	
			101496	Pte	Le Roy O. — wounded.	
			390	Pte	Mason J.M. — wounded at duty.	
		10 a.m.	156206	Pte	Weston E. — do	
			214	Pte	Plowright. E. — do	
			40030	Pte	Ellis J.J. — killed	
		9/10/17	9/10		Davis L.J. — killed.	
		do	10928	Pte	Yardley E. — killed.	
		do	951627	L.	Johnson R. — wounded.	
		5/10/17	8/10	46789	Pte	Dunn — 15 — wounded	
		6/10/17	8/10	35451	L/pl	Hodgkiss J.A. — wounded	
		do	12391	L.Cpl	Lawrence C.J. — wounded —	
		do	9/10	65715	Rpl	Kirk J. — killed	
		do	do	82983	L.Cpl	Hopper. J. — wounded.	
		do	9/10	31180	Pte	Smith J.H. — wounded.	

Army Form C. 2118.

WAR DIARY
or
INTELLIGENCE SUMMARY.
(Erase heading not required.)

CASUALTIES. OCTOBER 1917.

Place	Date	Hour	No	RR	Name	Summary of Events and Information	Remarks and references to Appendices
In the Field	7/10/17	a.m.	302218	Sgt	Blackburn. b	Returned wounded	
	do	do	241875	a/Sgt	Whalley. a	wounds at duty.	
		p.m.	103196	Pr	Martin. S.	wounded.	
			302865	do	Armstrong. J.L.	wounded	
			242095	do	Rhodes. H.	wounded	
			555209	do	Popson. H	wounded	
	do	a.m.		Pr	Edwards	wounded	
	do	do		Pr	Robinson	wounded	
	do	do	162100	Pr	Lockheart. R	missing since 4/10/17	
	do	p.m.		Pr	Thorer	wounded	
	do	do		Pr	Beilby	wounded	
	8/10/17	a.m.	36003	Cpl	Gornage. a	wounded	
			122661	a/Sgt	Edwards. J.J.	wounded	
			229306	Bdr	Gordon. a	wounded	
				Pr	Allen. g	wounded.	
		a.m.	92655	Pr	Gilroy. J	wounded.	
		a.m.	162180	do	Yayre. Sd	killed.	
			63913	do	Bell. K	wounded. b	
			1490				

Army Form C. 2118.

WAR DIARY
or
INTELLIGENCE SUMMARY.
(Erase heading not required.)

Instructions regarding War Diaries and Intelligence Summaries are contained in F. S. Regs., Part II. and the Staff Manual respectively. Title pages will be prepared in manuscript.

A.V. BL. R.F.A.

CASUALTIES OCTOBER 1917

Place	Date	Hour	No	R.R.	Name	Summary of Events and Information	Remarks and references to Appendices
In the Field	8/10/17	P.M.	190110	3/Sgt 3th	Poole	wounded	
		A.M.	227567	R/Bdr	Jackson J.S.	wounded	
			90818	Gr	William R.	wounded	
			816515		Lloyd's A.A.	wounded	
		B/24	20186	Sgt	Dobbins R.J.	wounded	
			33554	Fr	Bragg C.J.A.	wounded	
			961989	Br	Green S	wounded	
		B/94	876.07	Gr	Fish W.S.	wounded	
	10/10/17	A/94	165400	Cpl	Metcalfe A.H.	wounded (gas)	
			9318	Bdr	Beaut S	wounded (shellshock)	
			104410	Gr	Fletcher A	wounded on duty	
			85523	Gr	Shoveton C.J.	wounded	
		B/94	10957	Bdr	Bramage J.J.	killed	
		A/94	437200	Gr	Thompson H.	wounded on duty	
			48044	Gr	Stewart a	wounded	
			35094	Gr	Bell R.	wounded	
		B/94	10536	Bdr	Thompson IS	wounded	
			9137	Gr	James 15	wounded	
	12/10/17		59905	Gr	Mitchell G	wounded	

Army Form C. 2118.

WAR DIARY
or
INTELLIGENCE SUMMARY.
(Erase heading not required.)

O ∠ B.N.R.A.

CASUALTIES OCTOBER 1917

Place	Date	Hour	No	Rk	Name	Summary of Events and Information	Remarks and references to Appendices
In the Field	10/10/17	2 Pm	236315	Dr	Harwood. J	wounded	
		4 pm	675335	Dr	Keymer. R	wounded	
	11/10/17	4 Pm	236539	Dr	McNamara. P.	severe	
		8 pm	350048	Dr	Smith. A	wounded	
			85173	Dr	Rye. C.J.	wounded	
	14/10/17	9 pm	219116	Dr	Bertram. J	wounded	
		8 pm	840040	Dr	Eugene. L.R.	killed	
			122072	Dr	Pope. G.E.	killed	
	15/10/17	9 pm	125851	Dr	D'Orsa. G	wounded on duty	
			191028	Dr	Neil. A	wounded	
		9 am	198774	Dr	Gorman. C.A.	wounded (Gas)	
			8183	Dpl	Bayho. J.S.	wounded do	
			294461	Dr	Onfley. A.J	wounded (Gas)	
				Dr	Bon	wounded (Gas)	
	16/10/17	8 am	82973	Dr	Clarke. A.N	wounded (Gas)	
			163758	Dr	Zurre. S	wounded (Gas)	
	17/10/17	8 am	39347	Dr	Williard. R	wounded (Gas)	
			172785	Dr	Payne. Q.A.	wounded (Gas)	

Army Form C. 2118.

WAR DIARY
or
INTELLIGENCE SUMMARY.
(Erase heading not required.)

OCTOBER 1917

Place	Date	Hour	N.O.	Rk.	Name	Summary of Events and Information	Remarks and references to Appendices
						Casualties	
	18/10/17	B/Bn	177,91	Pte	Topp. P	wounded (Gas)	
	18/10/17		31	Sgt	Forsyth. J	wounded (Gas)	
	18/10/17	A/Bn	34657	Pte	Simpson. N. H	wounded (Gas)	
			37121	Pte	Seagrove. J	wounded - Gas.	
				Pte	Lawson	wounded (Gas)	
			33103	Pte	Kirkbridge. J	wounded (Gas)	
			37137	Pte	Parker. C. B.	wounded (Gas)	
	3/10/17	A/Pn	20524	Cpl	Henry. J	wounded (Gas)	
			117184	Bdr	Edwards. J.W	wounded (Gas)	
			62299	A/B	Carlin B	wounds &c	
	23/10/17	21 Bn	179315	Pte	Simpson. H.S	injured	
	24/10/17-M/Bn	37132	Cpl	Bailie	wounds	
	24/10/17	M/Bn	303365	Cpl	Parkinson. M	wounded (Gas)	
		do	765115	2/Lt	Atkinson E	wounded	
		do	36930	Pte	Ward. L	wounded (Gas)	
		do	1654	Pte	Barnes. J	wounded (Gas)	
	24/10/17	A/Bn	276109	Pte	Dixon. P.E	wounded (Gas)	
			155843	Pte	Rawle. P. J	wounded (Gas)	

Army Form C. 2118.

WAR DIARY
or
INTELLIGENCE SUMMARY.

G.K. Bde R.F.A

CASUALTIES OCTOBER 1917

Place	Date	Hour	No	Rk	Name	Summary of Events and Information	Remarks and references to Appendices
In the Field	24/10/17	2PM	40731	Dvr	Jones J.E.M	wounded (Gas)	
			30297	Dvr	Wilkinson J	wounded (SOS) attacks from TM Bde.	
	25/10/17	9PM	36675	Dvr	Hunt E	wounded (Gas)	
			63678	Sgt	Slack B.	wounded (Gas)	
			46618	Lt	Esperle J	wounded Gas — attacks from TM Bde.	
				Bpl	Cumpiece J	wounded Gas	
				Dvr	Rumney J	missing	
		8PM	36193	Dvr	Gill	wounded — attacked	
		8PM		Dvr	Marshall	wounded Trench mortar	
				Dvr	York	wounded Bde	
				Dvr	Giling	wounded activity	
	26/10/17	8PM	64773	Sgt	Randell A.S.	wounded	
				Bdr	Thackery S	wounded	
			9314187	Dvr	Kingham S	wounded	
			1847	Dvr	Clarke W.O.	wounded	
				Dvr	Royston	wounded Gas	
	29/10/17	9PM	37266	Sgt	Edds R.J	wounded Gas	
			35183	Bdr	Kindred E.R	wounded Gas	
			27203	Gnr	Brewer L	wounded Gas	

Army Form C. 2118.

WAR DIARY
INTELLIGENCE SUMMARY.
(Erase heading not required.)

Instructions regarding War Diaries and Intelligence Summaries are contained in F. S. Regs., Part II. and the Staff Manual respectively. Title pages will be prepared in manuscript.

CASUALTIES OCTOBER 1917

Place	Date	Hour	N.D.	R.D.	Name	Summary of Events and Information	Remarks and references to Appendices
	29/10/17		133690	Pte	Smith R.M.B.	wounded G.	
			40922	Pte	Smith G.	wounded G.	
			11280	Pte	Bradshaw D	wounded G.	
			139433	Pte	Rogers J.	wounded G.	
			32438	Pte	Jackson J.J.	wounded G.a.	
			42654	265	Mathe J	wounded (G.)	
			82286	Pte	Spoon B	wounded (Gas)	
			88969	Pte	Dotson W	wounded. G.	
			34436	Cpl	Howe L	wounded G.	
			53095	Sgt	Bucket J.G.	wounded G.	
			111722	R.M.	Johnson A.	wounded G.O.	
			220653	Pte	Rose	wounded G.	
			5855	Pte	Howard S.H.	wounded G.	
			92696	Pte	McIntosh 16	wounded G.	
	30/10/17	B/10/5	130050	Sgt	Sherwin B.H.	wounded G.O.	
		B/20/10		R.M.	Burke.	wounded G.	
			53654	Pte	Cole. O.B.	wounded G.	
			34869	Pte	adam J.D.	wounded G.	
			23815	Pte	Jacobs W.C.	wounded G.	
		B/14	19887	St.	Kennedy P.	wounded G.	

Army Form C. 2118.

WAR DIARY
or
INTELLIGENCE SUMMARY.
(Erase heading not required.)

94 Bde RFA

CASUALTIES OCTOBER 1917.

Place	Date	Hour	No	Rk	Name	Summary of Events and Information Nature	Remarks and references to Appendices
In the Field	30.10.17	2/Lt	802295	Bmr	Oxley. J.S.	Killed	
		2/Lt	915187	Br	Legris. J.R.	Wounded	
		21a	65574	Bpl	Murry. J	Wounded (Gas)	
		"	36347	Bpl	Heatherton. A	Wounded (Gas)	
		"	34781	Br	Harrow. A	Wounded (Gas)	
			154205	Br	Purcell. A.R.	Wounded (Gas)	
	31/10/17	2/Lt	196?	Br	Adam. V.S.	Wounded (Gas)	
		2/Lt	169598	Br	Gibson. H	Wounded (Gas)	
			85413	Sgt	King. W.C.	Wounded (Gas)	
			105069	Sgt	Goodall. F	Wounded (Gas)	
			7103		Gibson. J.H.	Wounded (Gas)	
		8/Lt	47251	Bdr	Prince. B.H.	Wounded (Gas)	
	31/10/17		30272	Br	Osborne. J	Wounded	

A. A. Loge Lt Col. RFA
Comdg. 94th Brigade R.F.A.

91st Brigade WAR DIARY R.F.A.

INTELLIGENCE SUMMARY.

November 1917

Vol 27

Army Form C. 2118.

Place	Date	Hour	Summary of Events and Information	Remarks and references to Appendices
No 6a 5 DORMY HOUSE	1	5.15 am	Corps Barrage in accordance with 2nd DA Order No 13	Sheet maps N/W Ypres
	4	5.45 am	Corps Barrage " " " " 13.	
	5	4.50 am	Corps Barrage " " " " 13.	
	4/5		In preparation for future operations a gas shell bombardment was carried out by D Battery 91st and D Battery 95th - targets Enemy Roads J19a 90 & J18 2.9.7	
	6	6 am	The 5th Division attacked POLDERHOEK CHATEAU and not found strong resistance on line J16c 7.0 - J16d 0.2 - the CHATEAU & J16d 3.0.8.5 15.15 hours of H.A. Group consisting of 91st Bde & 95th Bde were assisted by the H.A. Bge DSO were placed at disposal of 5th Division for Creeping Barrage - Batteries employed were A/94, and Creeping Gas + 109½. In conjunction an attack on BECELAERE the heritages of A Group D/91 + D/95 this shoots of Bucks were for shells on a line J15c69 & J15a8.0. The attack was not successful. No objective were reached owing to enemy fire and our batteries were ordered to continue firing which was done until dark	2 Z Dro. Hole N16

Army Form C. 2118.

WAR DIARY or INTELLIGENCE SUMMARY

9th Brigade 2/RFA
November 1917

Place	Date	Hour	Summary of Events and Information	Remarks and references to Appendices
	7	5.30	Army moving in accordance with 2nd D.A. Instruction No.17	2nd DA Instr no.17
	8		Owing to the relief of the 9th Div Arty in the line – 58th Battery and 108th Battery were taken over in position by 99th – 95th who were not ready to begin their relief, completed at 12.30 am on 9th inst	
	9	6pm	Regrouping of Artillery. A Group became Right Group consisting of 95th + 95th Brigades under command of Col MA (Boys) DSO	2nd DA OO msg
	13		Right Group relieved in the line by the 14th Army Brigade RFA (Col E. St Johns DSO) and by 59th Div Arty. Positions were re-organised making them into 4 gun and 2 gun positions, necessitating considerable labour in transferring guns from position to position. The command passed at 10.30 am to 14th Army Brigade who reoccupied Headquarters at DORMY House. Brigade Ammunition in wagon lines at RENINGHELST	2nd DA OO No.90
	18		Brigade transferred to MORBECQUE and billeted for the night	HAZE-BROUCK 6th Army

2/D.A. CO. No. 95

Army Form C. 2118.

9th Brigade RGA 3

WAR DIARY
or
INTELLIGENCE SUMMARY.

Title pages November 1917

Place	Date	Hour	Summary of Events and Information	Remarks and references to Appendices
MONCHIAUX	17	night	Brigade marched to VENDIN-LES-BETHUNE and billeted for night 2nd DA AO Msg 3	HAZEBROUCK 5a
	18		Brigade marched to HOUDAIN and billeted for the night.	2nd DA AO Msg 11
	19		Brigade marched to ESTREE-COUCHIE 2nd DA AO Msg 94	
	20/pm		2nd Div Arty relieve 47th Divisional Artillery. 2 batteries only of this Brigade to go into line B/94 and D/94 relieving B/236 and D/236 respectively	2nd DA Msg 45
	22		Headquarters and A & C Btys moved from ESTREE & COUCHIE into billets in CAPELLE-FERMONT and TREVIN-CAPELLE. Brigade Headquarters at BREVIN-CAPELLE.	
	24		B and D/94 returned to the line, shooting over guns Kemtyne to G/170 and D/170 withdrawing personnel to wagon line	
	26		B and D/94 marched to new Buckets at BEAN and VANDERCOURT	
	30	3.30 pm	Motor lorries arrived to march all men to ARRAS. - All Batteries were then at Bulleby by 5.45 pm - Brigade ARRAS - Battalion not given	A2DA 00 Msg 99

Harlock Lt Col. RGA
Comng. 94th 15th RGA.

Army Form C. 2118.

WAR DIARY
or
INTELLIGENCE SUMMARY. NOVEMBER 1917.
(Erase heading not required.)

94 Bde RFA

Place	Date	Hour		No	Rk	Name	Summary of Events and Information	Remarks and references to Appendices
In the Field	1st	By		31864	Gnr	Jackson. S	Buried.	
				50438	Bdr	George. S.R	do	
				131231	Gnr	Houghton. J	do	
	2nd	A		636361	Gnr	McLennon. a.	do	
		B		45933	Cpl	Laflin. L.R.	do	
		C		108117	Gnr	Fairbrother 15	do	
		D		91673	Gnr	Mullen. J	do	
	3rd	D		21005	Sgt	Cater L.h	do	
				12745	Cpl	Singleton	do	
				845172	Gnr	Dye. E	do	
	4th	A		134867	Gnr	Riley 15	do	
				1407165	Gnr	Russell A.h	do	
		C		65924	Gnr	Davies C	do	
		D		6982	Gnr	Ramsey. J.	do	
		C		63920	Gnr	Robinson. a	do	
				105148		Traynor P	do	
	5th			27094		Simpson. W.G	do	
				105405		Grossmiano. J	do	
	6th	B		981965	Gnr	Hope. E.O	do	
				96576	Gnr	Bleakley. H	do	
		D		40547	Gnr	Robinson. P	do	

Army Form C. 2118.

WAR DIARY
or
INTELLIGENCE SUMMARY.
(Erase heading not required.)

NOVEMBER 1917

Place	Date	Hour			Summary of Events and Information	Remarks and references to Appendices
			CASUALTIES			
In the	6th	C	235606	Bm'r	Smith J	Grave
Field			175456	Gnr	Thomson J	do
			160446	Bm'r	Mann J.W.	do
			835160	Gr	Robinson G.A	do
			405919	Sjt	Nottingham C.W.	do
	7th	D	41117		Glendon	do
		B	175147	Gr	Kennedy S.	do
	8th	A	46643	Gr	Williamson R.	do
			636361		Gray O.	do
			239008		Stockdale J	do
		B	213075		Thomas O.	do
			20020	G/Bmr	Roberts J	Wounded At duty
			4363	Bm	Gill J	Severe
		C	92767	Gr	Munro M.D	do
			85113	Bn	King W.C.	do at duty
		D	83003	W/Gm	Swick J.S	do do
			876039	Sr	Durrant R.W.	Severe
			105495		Senior R.W.	do
			105579		Downey J.	do at duty
	10th	C	671196	Gr	Foot R.	do do
	5th		77754		Farley R.	do do
	3rd		81950	Sgt	Smith. A. (A.V.C)	Found dead in his bivouac
	24th		71494	G/Bmr	Turner. W.	wounded

1977 Nought to Col. R.F.A.
Commdg 94 ra B ie R.F.A.

94th Brigade WAR DIARY R.F.A.
or INTELLIGENCE SUMMARY.

Army Form C. 2118.

VM 28

December 1917.

Place	Date	Hour	Summary of Events and Information	Remarks and references to Appendices
In the field	1.		Orders received for the Brigade which had been resting overnight (3rd Div) at VICTORY CAMP & Batteries bivouacked near ARRAS on the ARRAS-St POL road, to march to BEAULENCOURT near BAPAUME. The night was spent in bivouac in an open field. Weather very cold & insufficient huts provided. DA.00.100.	Map St QUENTIN 18
	2		Brigade marched to BRUSLE & bivouaced for the night. DA.00.101. Covered standings for horses & Niscen huts for personnel.	
B/a. Hdqrs Ste EMILIE E24 C37	3		Brigade marched in 2 Wagon Lines (K 5.C.6.3) on ROISEL – Ste EMILIE road. Positions were reccied & dug south of EPEHY. All Batteries moved up into action during the night of 3/4th Dec 17. & covered the Right Brigade (110th Inf Bde) which had the previous night taken over the line between MALASSISE FARM & CATALET ROAD. Battery positions "A" F 13 a 77.20. "B" F 13 a 73.85 "C" E 12 d 99.10 and "D" F 13 a 98.37. 6 into 7 Batteries from right & left "A B C" with "D" superimposed over the whole front. DA.OO. 103.	570 S.R.
	5		O.P. in EPEHY (F.1.b.22) was occupied in conjunction with Infantry.	
	11		Forward guns provided by A & B Btys (one each) were placed in semi-concealed positions in EPEHY (F.1.b.15.40) to find with their sights in the event of the enemy breaking through, down THRUSH and CATALET VALLEYS.	
	13	6.30 pm	Task 7 S.O.S. 10 sheafs. Nothing observed either at O.P. or Batteries moving to front.	

Army Form C. 2118.

94th Brigade WAR DIARY or INTELLIGENCE SUMMARY.

December 1917

Place	Date	Hour	Summary of Events and Information	Remarks and references to Appendices
	19		Further test of S.O.S. signal. Apparent failure owing to Bty stores. Only one rocket was seen by O.P. & none at all by Batteries.	
	21/22		Harassing fire. Entire Brigade gone carried out throughout the night. Allotment of ammunition 100 rounds per Bty. S.A.A.0107	
	26		Position of "A" & "D" 275 RFA & "Bee RFA at E12.a.93 & E12.d.30.14 respectively taken over.	
	27		To occupy these positions guns transferred by Batteries as follows:- "A", "B", "C" & "D" 2 at D.12. "B" guns transferred to SAULCOURT.	

Cuthbertson
Major
Cmdg. 94th Bde R.F.A.

Army Form C. 2118.

WAR DIARY
or
INTELLIGENCE SUMMARY

9th Brigade R.F.A.

Dec. 1917

Place	Date	Hour	Summary of Events and Information	Remarks and references to Appendices
Casualties				
Field	10/12/17	2/Lieut	E. Smith wounded in action.	
"	21/12/17	46615	Gnr. H. Drane " " " (remained at duty.)	
"	28/12/17	23900	Gnr. R. Strike " " "	
Honors awarded				
Field	11/12/17	Capt.	H.T. Collived. Mentioned in Despatches.	
"	"	Lieut.	T. Scott " " "	
"	"	2Lt.	H. Bamford " " "	

Arthur Tippin
Major
Cmdg 9th Bde
R.F.A.

14th Bde R.F.A.

WAR DIARY January 1918, Army Form C. 2118.
or
INTELLIGENCE SUMMARY.
(Erase heading not required.)

VII 29

Place	Date	Hour	Summary of Events and Information	Remarks and references to Appendices
H.Q.	1		S.O.S. Lines of C/95 Bde taken over X.20.d.2.1 & X.20.c.9.0.3.5.	
	3		95" Bde withdrew from line – new S.O.S. lines taken over.	
ST EMILIE	4		Regt R.B. & Bde joined from J Bty R.H.A. & were granted to D Bty	
Eap. 6.37.	10		Capt. J.L. Muller M.C. rejoined the Bde, on return from infantry (wounded at Ypres) posted to B. Bty.	
62E.N.E.	12		S.O.S. lines of C Bty altered to X.20.c.35.70 – X.20.a.0.0.	
	15		An Infantry Raid was carried out on enemy post at X.20.b.95.50 started at 7.30 p.m. Arty Barrage was called on to engage 3 machine gun posts, in case raiding party was troubled from that source, as nothing was heard of raiding party up to 9.15 p.m. Infantry Commander located his output to larger required. word received at 2 a.m. from B'de Maj. that enemy menacy resonating be ready 4 a.m. "Ren had been picked up. All Batteries warned to be ready to take alert. At 4 a.m. "HEYTHORT POST" (North of LEMPIRE), Kemply of 1th Division on our Right was raided & men of "Queens" Regt. taken prisoners.	
	17			
	20		First Silent Period commenced at 8 a.m. during the evening 2 hours the use of telephone was prohibited	
	23		Silent period from 8 a.m. to 8 a.m. 24th. S.O.S. signal changed to 2 Red and 2 Green lights.	
	25		orders issued for the support of a raid to be carried out by 62 Rifles on 26th G.D.&L. Rist R.E. to be opened licol 2 ft 2, ant eventually cancelled.	

94th Bde R.F.A.

Army Form C. 2118.

WAR DIARY
or
INTELLIGENCE SUMMARY.

94th Bde R.F.A. January 1918.

(Erase heading not required.)

Instructions regarding War Diaries and Intelligence Summaries are contained in F. S. Regs., Part II. and the Staff Manual respectively. Title pages will be prepared in manuscript.

Place	Date	Hour	Summary of Events and Information	Remarks and references to Appendices
H.Q.	27.		Capt A.H. Hornby M.C. posted to Bde., went to B.H.Q. in place of Capt. F.B. Miller, M.C., evacuated.	
St EMILIE	29.		Test of S.O.S. signals at 8pm. Although all rockets had one very light were not distinct, and unfavourable reports were received	
E.21.d.37.				
62.c.N.E.			about Barfitt, Webster & Mellor arrived from Bow pond to A.B.C. Batteries respectively.	

Hornby
Lieut Col. R.F.A.
Comdg. 94th Bde R.F.A.

H.Q.
94TH BRIGADE.
R.F.A.
No. 3
Date 2.18

Army Form C. 2118.

WAR DIARY
or
INTELLIGENCE SUMMARY.

(Erase heading not required.)

Pt "B" R.F.A.

January 1918.

Place	Date	Hour	Summary of Events and Information	Remarks and references to Appendices
Field	6th	—	Honors & Awards. Major C.M. Taylor D/9th. awarded "M.C."	
	6th	—	41652 Sgt. B.S. Newman B/9th " "D.C.M."	
			Casualties "Nil"	

February 1918.   94th Brigade R.F.A.   Army Form C. 2118.

WAR DIARY
or
INTELLIGENCE SUMMARY.
(Erase heading not required.)

Vol 30

Place	Date	Hour	Summary of Events and Information	Remarks and references to Appendices
H.Q. ST EMILIE	1		Silent Period 8 a.m. to 8 p.m.	
	2		Bde Recce 'C' Bty was relieved in the line by 95th Bde R.F.A. (Leon C.B.Y.) and withdrew to wagon lines SAULCOURT for the purpose of training.	Bde order No 6
E.24.B.3.9.	5		B Bty calibrated guns at calibration Range Le QUINCONCE (sheet 62c.T.I)	
62c.N.E.	11		B Bty returned to their positions in the line in relief of C Bty, who withdrew to wagon lines at SAULCOURT.	sheet 62c. J.3.d.
DRIENCOURT	12		Wagon lines of H.Q., C, and D Bty moved to DRIENCOURT lately occupied by Nos. 2 and 3 sections 9/st B.A.C.	
			A Bty calibrated their guns at Le QUINCONCE.	
	13		A Bty moved wagon lines to DRIENCOURT.	
	14		C Bty calibrated their guns.	
	16		D Bty calibrated their guns.	
	17		Retaliative air raid carried out by enemy between 6.30 p.m. and midnight in district around TAMPLEUX-LA-FOSSE, DRIENCOURT N.E. TINCOURT and BUSSU. Between 250 and 300 bombs estimated to have been dropped.	sheet 62c
	19		A Bty occupied new wagon lines at LONGAVESNES and the name A Bty was returned to their positions in the line in relief of B Bty, who evening returned to their gun positions and wagon lines at SAULCOURT withdrew took from their rear gun positions and wagon lines at SAULCOURT back to DRIENCOURT for further training.	
	27		As a test of scheme for reinforcing the front in case of attack orders were received at 11.45 p.m. for Bde to move into action immediately. DRIENCOURT was cleared by 5.30 p.m. and the rendezvous (E.27 central) reached by 6.30 p.m. The Bde then came under the command of C.R.A. 16 Division from whom orders were received at 7.10 p.m. for Btys to occupy their late positions in the line.	

February 1918. 94th Brigade R.F.A.

Army Form C. 2118.

WAR DIARY
or
INTELLIGENCE SUMMARY.
(Erase heading not required.)

Instructions regarding War Diaries and Intelligence Summaries are contained in F.S. Regs., Part II. and the Staff Manual respectively. Title pages will be prepared in manuscript.

Place	Date	Hour	Summary of Events and Information	Remarks and references to Appendices
DRIENCOURT	27		Started again at 7.25pm and proceeding by VILLERS FAUCON Bde reached their position and were ready to fire on S.O.S. Zone by 8.45 pm. the Bde then returned to DRIENCOURT.	See order No 10.
	28		Bde moved at short notice from DRIENCOURT (which was shelled by 4.30pm) to new wagon lines LONGAVESNES and went into action the same evening in support of 110th Infantry Bde. B Bty took up a new position about E.17.a.6.0. and D Bty returned to those which they had previously occupied, with the exception that D Bty put their detached section into B Bty's late main position instead of "Dx" as formerly.	
			Honors and Awards.	
Field	29/1/18		No.45901. Sergt. W. Davis D Bty awarded Croix de Guerre (Belgian) No 78665 Bomdr G. Owens C Bty awarded Croix de Guerre (Belgian)	
			Casualties	
"	19/2/18		No. 35289. Bgbr A Hallam B Bty wounded in action. G.S.W.	

A.M. Vogt
Lt Col RFA
Comdg 94th Bde R.F.A.

H.Q.
94TH BRIGADE.
R.F.A.
No.............
Date 2.3.18

21st Div.

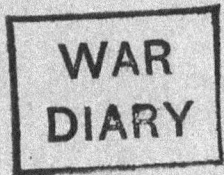

Headquarters,

94th BRIGADE, R.F.A.

M A R C H
(13/30.3.18)
1 9 1 8

GHA 95 Brigade R.H.A.

WAR DIARY
or
INTELLIGENCE SUMMARY.
(Erase heading not required.)

March 1918   Army Form C. 2118.

VA 31

Place	Date	Hour	Summary of Events and Information	Remarks and references to Appendices
HQ St EMILIE	13th		Artillery support was given by "D" Bty to a successful raid carried out by 2nd Royal Munster Fusiliers (16th Div:) at midnight 13th/14th.	
	13/14		"B" Battery having been selected as training Battery for 5th Army Artillery School, were relieved in the line by "B"/95th Brigade R.F.A. They endeavour to their wagon lines LONGAVESNES overnight and commenced their side days at 9 a.m. 14.3.18.	
	16	11.30pm	All Batteries gave the protection of their guns to a party of the 6th Bn. Leicester Regiment (21st Division) who carried out a successful raid on enemy's trenches about (Sheet 62.c N.E.) x.21.f. Prisoners were captured and rest of the garrison killed without casualty to our men who were back in our trenches by midnight.	
	21		Between 4.30 and 4.45 am the preparatory bombardment of the great German offensive began. Owing to the 16th Division on our right being forced back and our encirclement	

Army Form C. 2118.

WAR DIARY
or
INTELLIGENCE SUMMARY.
(Erase heading not required.)

Instructions regarding War Diaries and Intelligence Summaries are contained in F. S. Regs., Part II. and the Staff Manual respectively. Title pages will be prepared in manuscript.

Place	Date	Hour	Summary of Events and Information	Remarks and references to Appendices
Continued.	21st		Thereby being checked. Batteries were withdrawn during the afternoon to previously selected positions at SAULCOURT. "A" Battery was transferred to SAULCOURT–LONGAVESNES Road, were only able to get one gun away, the remainder falling into the hands of the enemy.	Sheet 62 c N.E.
DUR SAULCOURT– LONGAVESNES Road		2200	Orders were received about 11 a.m. that the Corps were withdrawing to BROWN LINE, with a switch from SAULCOURT to TINCOURT WOOD to protect our Right flank. The Brigade withdrew at once to positions just N. of BIZECOURT LE BAS in accordance with 21st Divisional Artillery orders. At 5 p.m. half Batteries retired by order of 21st Divisional Artillery to previously selected positions for defence of GREEN LINE, at N.E. end of BUSSU WOOD. The remainder were to retire at 6 p.m. but owing to the speedy advance of the enemy 8/9th Brigade, the whole team were up, was forced to take up intermediate positions at N. end of EPINETTE WOOD and from there

Place	Date	Hour	Summary of Events and Information	Remarks and references to Appendices

Sd

BUSSU — 23rd —

LIERAMONT: As teams were not up to Dronsiger belonging to D/9th Brigade R.F.A. had to be abandoned lights and breech blocks were removed. At 5pm the remainder of 61gw retired and rejoined the Bgd near BUSSU WOOD. H.Q. rested in BUSSU overnight. Brigade received orders at 6 am to withdraw and take up new positions West of PERONNE-BOUCHAVESNES line. At the request of the G.O.C. 6xth Infantry Brigade, Batteries remained in action until 9.15 am to cover retirement of Infantry from GREEN LINE. Each position were taken up just behind MOUNT ST QUENTIN, and all Batteries were in action again by 11am. Up to nightfall there engaged the enemy on WEST edge of Bouchavesnes. O.P's so likely places of assembly W. of Deleincourt were fired on. Just after noon the accuracy of enemy came into view and were engaged continually until 3pm when a further attack became menacing owing to the presence of the enemy in PERONNE and the fact that MOUNT ST QUENTIN could not be cleared at short range: orders had been received from 20th Divisional Artillery at 2.30pm that the next line of resistance would be CLERY- BOUCHAVESNES and gun positions on line HEM-MAUREPAS-N of the Brigade area commenced at about 3 pm. Roads were

WAR DIARY
or
INTELLIGENCE SUMMARY

Army Form C. 2118.

Place	Date	Hour	Summary of Events and Information	Remarks and references to Appendices

went forward, progress being reduced to not more than 1 mile per hour and enemy aircraft kept me very active with machine guns, but with remarkably little effect. Railways stopped into action just N. of NALLE (I.13.a) to engage at extreme range enemy infantry advancing from just PALAINES. Very effective shooting was done that gun observation could once confirm of Batteries. Batteries withdrew further in the evening and got into action N.E. of GURLU by midnight. In this day one gun under LIEUTENANT CHAPMAN, who was unable to ascertain the situation, were coming up via PERONNE to replace casualties in B/92d when near PERONNE it was observed that our own infantry had retired and lines of enemy infantry were advancing in full view. Lt. CHAPMAN at once brought his gun into action with open sights firing all at ammunition in gun limbers during considerable evacuation at get gun away without mishap. He reports he Baker's dump the night making the orders of the day 3 howitzers joined "D" Battery B/92d 1 gun D/92 5 guns D/92. 6 howitzers up to the following: — not yet rejoined from 5th Army artillery school, owing to poor visibility the enemy did not come into view.

2nd/3rd/Sept.

MARICOURT

94th Bde. R.F.A.

Diary 24th March 1918

For "B.24.c.", "B.22."
& "B.20.c."
Read "A.24.c.", "A.22"
& "A.20.c."

25.10.26   H M Davies

WAR DIARY
or
INTELLIGENCE SUMMARY.

(Erase heading not required.)

Army Form C. 2118.

Place	Date	Hour	Summary of Events and Information	Remarks and references to Appendices
	25		until 9 a.m. From that time until noon, during which our own infantry continued to retire steadily, troops the enemy were continually engaged by all guns of the Brigade. About noon the Brigade retired by order of 5th Divisional Artillery to positions about R.24.c. and subsequently to R.23.d. At about 6.30pm our infantry (now 35th Division) were holding a line about 1000 yards East of MARICOURT and the Bulgars who withdrew to positions about B.30.c. (35th Divisional Artillery order). Brigade remained in action all day covering infantry line E of MARICOURT. This line already heavily attacked was maintained South and East of village and driven back onwards North of it. At 8 p.m. orders for retirement were received and the Brigade moved about 10 p.m. to E.23 marching via SUZANNE and BRAY Road. "A" Battery remained in action till 2 a.m. 26th and maintained an unceasing rapid rate of fire so as to hide the withdrawal of other Batteries. Prior to this retirement M.95, D/95 and G/9ad were withdrawn from the line, handing over their guns to remaining Batteries of 2nd Divisional Artillery which	x x x

WAR DIARY or INTELLIGENCE SUMMARY

Army Form C. 2118.

Place	Date	Hour	Summary of Events and Information	Remarks and references to Appendices
	26		Came under D/A 9th Bde Brigade R.F.A. D/A 95th Brigade R.F.A. were withdrawn from the line. Batteries were in action by 5.30 a.m. 10 pm in K.23.a and B/94 in enemy sight of 29 central covering the runway to new across the ANCRE and was unable to open the crossing at TREUX. Battalions were at in action by 2 pm B/94 in D.10.a and H.5 howitzer in D.17.c. On this day B/94 rejoined the Brigade from 5th Army Artillery School and came into action in D.16.a. D/A was bivouacked at D.9 central (approx). Further retirement was ordered from the north so our infantry succeeded in holding the line of the railway between DERNANCOURT and BUIRE. Visibility greatly improved from this date and an enlarged dump batteries had most successful shoots on concentrations of the enemy such good observations.	
	29		B/94, D/94 and D/A 94th Brigade R.F.A. were relieved by the combined units of the 95th Brigade R.F.A. and retired to BAIZIEUX. B/94 was relieved in the line by C/95 and switched to BEAUCOURT to which the rest of Brigade R.F.A. / (less B/94) had previously retired.	
	30			

Army Form C. 2118.

WAR DIARY
or
INTELLIGENCE SUMMARY.
(Erase heading not required.)

Instructions regarding War Diaries and Intelligence Summaries are contained in F.S. Regs., Part II. and the Staff Manual respectively. Title pages will be prepared in manuscript.

Place	Date	Hour	Summary of Events and Information	Remarks and references to Appendices
	31/3/18		Casualties	
			"A" Battery.	
			2/Lieut. C. J. Norman. wounded	
			44673 Bdr. R. Gee "	
			65112 Gnr. R. Youngson "	
			75184 " O. Pondon "	
			2216 " Ja. Steward "	
			11697 " G.W. Cawey "	
			34260 " W. Snigg. "	
			170213 " W. Roberts missing	
			"B" Battery	
			62978 Bdr. Ger. Sankill wounded	
			22850 Dvr. J.W. Heath "	
			93133 Gnr. G.W. Lamb. "	
			67196 " R. Drove "	
			223519 " J. Bryant " Severe	
			35086 Dvr. J. Lawler "	
			"D" Battery	
			Lieut. B.B. Edge wounded	
			2/Lieut. J.A. Ruston "	
			837 Gnr. F. Kent "	
			79361 Gnr. K. Wallace "	
			80193 " J. Ball "	
			965018 2/Bdr. R. Oakley Killed in action	
			55496 Gnr. W.H. Wilson died of wounds	

WAR DIARY or INTELLIGENCE SUMMARY

Army Form C. 2118.

(Erase heading not required.)

Place	Date	Hour	Summary of Events and Information	Remarks and references to Appendices
	27/3/18		"A" Battery.	
			42379 Dr. A. Rommel Killed in action.	
			35576 Dr. J. Friet Wounded	
			97060 Dr. E.B. Martin " "	
			"C" Battery.	
			78665 Bdr. G. Snow Wounded	
			1927m Gnr. A. Manning " (at duty).	
			19630 " J. Egnardy " "	
			186716 " D. Knighton " "	
	23.		"B" Battery	
			190919 Gnr. A. Daley Missing.	
			74623 Cpl. Jr. J. Fielder Wounded.	
			Y Kent W.H. BURFITT in — (at duty).	
			"A" Battery.	
			34238 Hyr. E. Blackburn Wounded.	
	27.		851622 Gnr. J. Keeley Killed in action.	
			220122 " W. Dunnett " "	
			220128 " Jr. Snag " "	
			169663 " W. Andrews Wounded C.	
			"D" Battery	
			125 SFg Bgr. F. Tierney. Wounded (at duty).	

WAR DIARY or INTELLIGENCE SUMMARY

Army Form C. 2118.

Place	Date	Hour	Summary of Events and Information	Remarks and references to Appendices
	29/3/18		"B" Battery 2/Lieut. E.M.V.Spath. Killed in action. 34287 Gnr. N. Batt. wounded, 63640 Dvr. W. Tallent " "	
			Headquarters 341826 Spr. J.Miles to wounded	
	27		3529 Dvr. J. Price wounded 7326 Gnr. A. Cutter " Capt. B.J. Mullin. R.A.M.C. "	
	28		26012.12. Pnr. W. Webb. died of wounds. — N.K. [signature] Hanlon Honours and Rewards. Lieut Col RFA Comdg 92nd Brigade RFA	

21st Divisional Artillery.

94th BRIGADE R.F.A. ::: APRIL 1918.

94th Bde R.F.A.

Army Form C. 2118.

WAR DIARY
or
INTELLIGENCE SUMMARY
(Erase heading not required.)

April 1918

Place	Date	Hour	Summary of Events and Information	Remarks and references to Appendices
BEAUCOURT	1		The Rear B Battery in rest at BEAUCOURT. B Battery who had remained in action under o/c 95th Bde R.F.A. in position S.E. of BRESLE were withdrawn from the line and rested overnight in their wagon lines at BAIZIEUX	See 62D
	2		The Brigade went into billets at FRECHENCOURT. H.Q. remained at BEAUCOURT-sur-HALLUE	
	4.		The Brigade came under the Command of 4th Australian Division and at 4.30 pm, to position of observation N.W. of CORBIE. Battery positions were astride I 26 and 32, and covered the front between VAIRE - sur - CORBIE and the Bois de VAIRE - held by 4th Australians. H.Q. at ESSARDONNEUSE	
			wagon lines at QUERRIEU	See notes
	6		The Brigade came under the command of 3rd Australian Division	
	9		The Brigade was relieved & went to wagon lines	
	11		The Brigade marched at 9.am QUIZANCOURT near DOULLENS where it was in BdeR	2nd A.D.O.O.
H.Q. at Q33.4.5.5.	13/14		The Brigade entrained at DOULLENS and detrained at GODNEARSVELDE from where it was taken by N. of FLETRE in W.14, 5, and 6, and was under the tactical control of 133 French Division and superimposed over the front S.W. of METEREN. Wagon lines in P.7, 17, and 24.	See 28
H.Q. at R.18.6.4.4	19		Brigade moved with H.Q. 133 Heads position to a sector further North, and Batteries went into action N. of MONT ROUGE and were superimposed on front N. of BAILLEUL. Wagon lines near WESTOUTRE	See 27 See 28
H.Q. at R.20.C	23		Moved overnight 23/24 to position S.W. of BERTHEN and carried the name wagon lines as before. Near GODNEARSVELDE	See 27

WAR DIARY
INTELLIGENCE SUMMARY

Army Form C. 2118.

9th Bgde R.F.A.

April 1918

Place	Date	Hour	Summary of Events and Information	Remarks and references to Appendices
Field	10		Casualties	
	19		H. Paul, R. Simmons A/94 wounded in action "Gas"	
			30488 Br. Enoch S. 5/94 "	
	20		55737 — Annie R " "	
	"		115615 Br. Kirk ? ?P — Killed in action	
	"		71107 — Mackin E.G. "	
	"		765365 — Arnot W. "	
	25		91979 Sgt. [?] W.R. wounded in action "Shell Shock"	
	"		15207 A/By Hendry H. "	
	"		16614 Br. Ross E.C. "	
	"		[?] [?] "	
	"		[?] [?]	
	"		Major F.R.W. Fraser [?]	
	16		165793 sgt McInnes R. 2/94 "	
	23		57643 S/S Smith D. 3/94 "	
	"		Lt. Micaela? 4/94 "	
	"		41503 Br Byers C. A/94 killed in action	
	"		128011 Gnr Johnston L. " wounded in action 31.5.18	
	29		92994 " Hay F. A/94 died of wounds	
	"		125487 Driver Hart E. 94 Killed in action	
	21		7861. W.T. Caylor 5/94 "	
	"		283141 Gnr McKim E.C. " [?] in action	
	"		270713 Gnr Riley A5, "	
	"		41128 L. Boyd A. "	
	"		78354 — Daniel "	
	"		5117 L. H. Hill "	

Army Form C. 2118.

WAR DIARY
or
INTELLIGENCE SUMMARY.

(Erase heading not required.)

9th Bde R.A. April 1918

Place	Date	Hour	Summary of Events and Information	Remarks and references to Appendices
Field			Honours and Awards	
			6.247809 Bgl. E.C. Sampio H.Q awarded Bar to Military Medal	
			1702 13 Gnr Leslie A/94 " " Military Medal	
			-31260 Dr D.G. Grigg " " " "	
			43657 Sgt. T. Burtles C/94 " " " "	
			35343 Bgl. H. E. Chant " " " " "	
			35383 Dr G Stanton " " " " "	
			44621 Dr W.J. Dean " " " " "	
			45114 Dr R. Jones " " " " "	
			186114 Bdr. W.J. Fowler D/94 " " " "	
			747068 Bgl. B.R. Allen " " " " "	
			46510 Bdr J.H. Haydon " " " " "	
			121860 Gnr W.W. Terrott " " " " "	
			27555 Gnr B Mayles " " " " "	
	8.5.18			

Ian Noyd
Lieut Col. R.F.A.
Comdg 9th Bde R.F.A.

Army Form C. 2118.

WAR DIARY
or
INTELLIGENCE SUMMARY.
(Erase heading not required.)

9th May 1918

Vol 33

Place	Date	Hour	Summary of Events and Information	Remarks and references to Appendices
BERTHEN	1		Batteries in action S.W. of BERTHEN covering the front held by 133rd French Div. H.Q. on Northern slopes of MONT DES CATS. Wagon Line GODNEARSVELDE British	
BLEROT	4		Lifters were given by Batteries to a local enterprise carried out by 133rd French Div. in the early morning, which proved successful. About noon Batteries pulled out and moved to ST MOMELIN near ST OMER and remained for the night.	(SOISSONS map)
	5		All Batteries arrived at ARQUES and WIZERNES	
	6/7		Returned at SERTY et PRIN and marched to Rest Camps at LHERY	
	13		All Ammunition for LHERY at 11 am STRIGNY, and went into Rest stage Camps	
	15		All Brigade relieved the 7th French Divl Arty in the sector now occupied. N. of LOIVRE Batteries took up positions in the vicinity of HERMONVILLE and CAUROY. HQ at STAUBOEUF Wagon Lines remained at TRIGNY.	
	18		Lines moved to Camps about 1 mile S. of BOUVANCOURT on the BOUVAN COURT-JONCHERY Road	
	26		As a result of news from prisoners of an impending enemy attack counter preparation fire was carried out by all Batteries from 10 pm May [26?]. HE and Gas shell bombardment opened at 1 am by enemy from zero and HQ's from the commencement of enemy's barrage, Batteries continuing to fire on "Z" Barrage line until 8 am when as the request of F.O.C. 6115 infantry Batts, fire was changed to "V" barrage.	
	27		Owing to the progress being made by the enemy, mainly the ground N. and E. of Batteries to Brigade had to retreat positions on to high ground N. of STAUBOEUF, was commenced at 11.30 am. The last Bty were withdrawn about 3 pm and all Batteries were in action again in their new positions by 6 pm. Barrages were commenced at 8.30 pm, and took up positions in the vicinity of TRIGNY.	

WAR DIARY
INTELLIGENCE SUMMARY

94th Brigade R.F.A.

May 1918

Place	Date	Hour	Summary of Events and Information	Remarks and references to Appendices
	28		The enemy were reported at 10 a.m. to be nearing the Great W. of TRIGNY, (H Bn Order C2.) so A and C Batteries who were not clear of that range were ordered to positions near CHALONS-sur-VESLE, slightly S.O. of the Infantry Bde. when for a barrage between BUTTE de PROUILLY and R. VESLE it was thought to be done. It was necessary to also withdraw B and D Batteries to positions W. of CHALONS-sur-VESLE. About 12.30 p.m. the news received from 21 D.A. that no position could be W. of ROSNAY. As this position was most suitable for the task in hand, B Batteries were ordered to ROSNAY at once, the remaining Bty following at intervals of about 1 hour. Suitable positions were found by all Batteries and effective work was done	SOISSONS Map.
	29		A C.B. group was obviously about midday when a further withdrawal had to be commenced owing to the proximity of the enemy who were gaining ground rapidly on our left flank in the direction of TRESLON. Immediate positions were taken up about 4 mile N.W. of MERY PREMECY, viz. about 6 km when, after consultation with F.O.B. C 62 64, and 110 Infantry Bde., it was decided to withdraw all Batteries to the neighbourhood of VILLERS FARM, 1 mile S.W. of ST EUPHRAISE and cover TRESLON Ridge.	
	30		Batteries moved at about 4 am to position N.E. of BLIGNY, in covered 19th Division owing to the enemy advance from SARCY, and the retirement of our Infantry from that district, Batteries were forced to withdraw at about 11 am and came into action by order of 21 D.A. near POURCY during the afternoon Bns received from 21 D.A. early in the morning to act as [?] Battery in positions between COURMAS and the BDIS de PETIT CHAMP and cover the line between AUBILLY and BLIGNY Rwd by 25th French Divn. Positions were selected and reached by noon.	
	31		D Battery remained in their position near POURCY, because for the moment H.E. Howr ammunition was not available. Wagon Lines about half way between FLEURY and NANTEUIL.	

WAR DIARY or INTELLIGENCE SUMMARY

Army Form C. 2118.

94th Brigade R.F.A.

Place	Date	Hour	Summary of Events and Information	Remarks and references to Appendices
Armentières	May 1918			
	6		23821 Sgt. Garner G. awarded Military Medal B/94	
			9099 — " Kanlam W.B. " " " "	
	8		27555 Gnr. Maple J. " " " "	
	16		148617 Sgt. Cowdrey R.J. awarded D.C.M. B/94	
	19		2/Lieut Blaksam R.P. awarded D.S.O. A/94	
	"		Major Altrey C⁰. " Bar to Military Cross C/94	
	"		Capt. McLaird J⁰ " Military Cross A/94	
	"		Lieut. Murray Ryan O " " " D/94	
	"		2/Lieut Brompton W. " " " A/94	
	"		" Galleia J. " " " B/94	
	21		780141 Gnr. Robinson A. awarded Military Medal P/94	
			175953 2/Br. Ardsley N. " " " "	
			76389 Gnr. Vanbey W.A. " " " "	

Van Voyt
Lieut Col R.F.A.
Comdg 94th Brigade R.F.A.

Army Form C. 2118.

WAR DIARY
or
INTELLIGENCE SUMMARY.
(Erase heading not required.)

9th C.M.R. May 1918

Place	Date	Hour	Summary of Events and Information	Remarks and references to Appendices
France	27		Casualties	
			750178 Pte. Ray A. wounded in action Gas A/9th	
			227110 Cpl. Weaver J. " " " "	
			26508 " Blaikie J. " " " "	
			3336 " Fitzsimmons R. " " " "	
			68710 " Rupnow D. " " " "	
			115880 " Morris A. " " " "	
			Major Godfrey C.W. " " " C/9th	
			190285 Sjt. Patterson W.J. wounded in action C/9th (remained at duty)	
			82003 Cpl. Smith T.J. " " " "	
	5		210576 Gnr. Bowell J.B. " " " "	
	29		760634 " Long J.T. " " " "	
			309302 " Briggens C. " " " "	
			31627 " Box L. " " " "	
			82188 Bdr. Rankin T.A. " " " "	
			39763 Gnr. Eccles W.G. " " " "	
			891610 Gnr. Weaver H. " " " "	
			63613 " Cook J.G.R. " " " "	
			19650 Bdr. Palmer J.A. died of wounds "	
			23799 Gnr. Turner H. killed in action "	
			131089 Dr. Harvey J. " " " "	
			63551 Sjt. Ridge W.J. killed in action D/9th	
			565517 L/Sjt. Smith C.G. (A.C.) (remained in action) "	
			210578 Gnr. Wait R. " " "	
			760138 Dr. Perigoe D. " " "	
	29		21074 Bdr. Jones W.J. " " "	

9th Brigade R.F.A. War Diary (1) June 1918

A.F.C.2118 (M.S.)
VK 34

Place	Date	Hour	Summary of Events and Information	Remarks
	3rd		D Battery came forward into action in BOIS de REIMS alongside the other Batteries. All Battery wagon lines moved to ST. IMOGES.	Ref. Soissons Map Sheet 52
	5th		All Batteries moved back to appealing positions in the B. de POURCY.	
	14th		The Brigade was relieved at 11 p.m. by the 3rd group of the 228th French Regiment, and withdrew to wagon line.	
	15th		Brigade moved to GOINGES.	
	16th		Brigade moved to CONNANTRAY.	
	17th		Brigade moved to MAILLY le CAMP.	
	18th		Entrained at SOUDÉ-SUD.	
	19th		Detrained at LONGPRÉ.	
	20th		Moved to ERONDELLE area	
	21st		moved to BOULLAH COURT area.	
	23rd		moved to E.U.	
	30th		arrived at 9 a.m. at MARTAINVILLE area.	
	10th		Capt. etc	
			2/Lt G.P. Chapman D.S.O. wounded in action A Bty	
	1st		No. 763139 Gnr W. Pawley M.M. " " " "	
	5th		No. 60826 Sgt J. Rydon " " " "	
	1st		35037 Gnr J. McDougall " " " "	

A.F.C.W.18. M.S.

94th Brigade R.F.A. June 1918. War Diary (2.)

Place	Date	Hour	Summary of Events and Information	Remarks
	1st		Casualties contd. 141330 Bowr. Moran S. wounded in action	B Bty.
	5th		147743 — Salvidge H.A. "	"
	1st		127554 Dr. Foy Q. "	"
	9th		212316 Gnr. Lee W. "	"
			103720 Bdr. Eilman J. "	"
			82970 Bdr. Buick W. "	"
			239451 Sgt. Jameson W. "	"
			5008 — Parks F.F. "	C Bty.
	6th		177375 Gnr. Brotman C. "	S
	3rd		225-76 — A.M.kin S.S. "	"
	7th		45627 — Reed A. "	"
			147701 — Badland A. — (at duty)	

Honors & Awards.
P/R.M.G. Bromilow. awarded. M.C. B Bty.
R/Lt. J.A. Stitt. " " "
Gnr. J.W. Atkinson awarded M.M. — Sgt. J. White awarded M.M.
" J.W. Thompson " " — Gnr. C. Ross "
" R. Riddell " " — Bdr. J. A. Taylor "
" J. Arthur " "
" J.A. Brearly " "
" G. Watson " "
Bdr. W. Atkinson " "

J. Coney
Major R.F.A.
Comdg. 94th Bde R.F.A.

H.Q. 94th BRIGADE R.F.A
16.7.18.

War Diary

94th Bde R.F.A.
July 1918

Place	Date	Hour	Summary of Events and Information	Remarks
At Abbeville	1		Brigade at rest in VISMES-AU-VAL, where it became immobile owing to an epidemic of influenza.	ABBEVILLE MAP
	3		Moved to ERONDELLE, with the assistance of Ambulances and Motor Lorries. Temporary hospital erected here. As many as 200 all ranks were effected with influenza at one time.	
	22		Leaving ERONDELLE at 9.30 a.m. the Brigade marched to CANAPLES and was billeted for the night. (31st D.A. order No 30.)	
	23		Starting 9 a.m. the Brigade marched to neighbourhood of RAINCHEVAL. Horse Lines were situate in N.11.B. and N.12.a. Billets were obtained in RAINCHEVAL	Also 57 D.
H.Q. R.31.d.4.4 (R.57)	27		In accordance with 31 D.A. order No 32, the Brigade in the evening commenced the relief of 121 Brigade R.F.A.	Covering the HAMEL front of the V Corps.
	28		Lines moved to ACHEUX. Take over from 121 Brigade R.F.A. completed by 7 a.m. Much harassing fire carried out each night.	
	30		Bombardment of enemy's line, first with smoke shell commencing 9 a.m. followed at 9.10 for 15 minutes; and 9.55 for 5 minutes by Shrapnel and H.E. (31 D.A. order No 33).	

Casualties nil.
Honors/Awards nil.

H.Q. 94th BRIGADE, R.F.A.
3.8.18

Lt Col R.F.A.
Comdg 1st Bde R.F.A.

94th Bde R.F.A.
94 Bde R.F.A.
(1) Vol 36

WAR DIARY
INTELLIGENCE SUMMARY.

Army Form C. 2118.

Instructions regarding War Diaries and Intelligence Summaries are contained in F.S. Regs., Part II. and the Staff Manual respectively. Title pages will be prepared in manuscript.

(Erase heading not required.)

August 1918.

Place	Date	Hour	Summary of Events and Information	Remarks and references to Appendices
H.Q. P.24.d.3.5.	1st to 20th		The Bde covered the Right half of 12th Divl. front opposite HAMEL (Ancre) The Batteries were disposed in depth in the vicinity of ENGLEBELMER, at ranges varying from 3300 to 5000 yards from the enemy lines. All Batteries had a detached section in forward positions, and from these a great deal of harassing fire was carried out by night and day. In the early part of the month the targets engaged mostly were the crossings of the River ANCRE opposite the Divisional front, and the roads leading thereto. Later, after the enemy had been forced to evacuate HAMEL fire was directed on trenches, roads, and tracks round THIEPVAL, THIEPVAL WOOD, and ST PIERRE DIVION	Sheet 57D Sheet 57D
	20		With a view to offensive operation, Batteries were moved forward to positions in the valley running northwards from MESNIL Q.22 and 28. One section of B/94 was left in later Red previously been its forward position, from which three all harassing fire detailed for the Brigade was carried out	
	21/24		The Infantry attack, which commenced in the early morning of the 21st were only partially successful until the morning of 24th when the 64th Infantry Bde succeeded in establishing themselves on the high ground South of MIRAUMONT, after forcing a crossing of the River ANCRE at GRANDCOURT. This advance placed all Batteries out of range, and orders were consequently issued by 21 D.A. for the Brigade to proceed to positions of readiness, which had been reconnoitered the previous day on the Western slopes of ARTILLERY VALLEY in R.2.a and c. Owing to the broken state of the Roads through BEAUMONT HAMEL and BEAUCOURT and the probability of congestion there, Btys were moved at intervals of about 2 hours, commencing with B Bty at 10.30 a.m., followed in order by C.D.A.	Sheet 57D

Army Form C. 2118.

WAR DIARY
or
INTELLIGENCE SUMMARY. (2)

9th A. Bde R.F.A.

August 1918.

(Erase heading not required.)

Instructions regarding War Diaries and Intelligence Summaries are contained in F.S. Regs., Part II. and the Staff Manual respectively. Title pages will be prepared in manuscript.

Place	Date	Hour	Summary of Events and Information	Remarks and references to Appendices
H.Q. P.24.d.3.5.	21/24		B and C Btys were reported ready to fire from new positions by about 11.30 p.m. Before Dark A Bty arrived in the new divisional area received that our Infantry had made a further advance, and were within a few hundred yards of the BAPAUME – ALBERT Road N. of LE SARS. The positions in ARTILLERY VALLEY thus placed out of range. After consultation with the G.O.C. 62nd Inf. Bde. it was decided to come into action behind the crest on the High ground S. of MIRAUMONT by dawn the following morning to support an attack on LE SARS. The night was therefore spent under cover in ARTILLERY VALLEY without A and D Btys coming into action.	See 157 D
H.Q. R.10.b.2.8.	25		About dawn positions were selected on and near N. MIRAUMONT Road about R11 central and batteries were all in action by 7 am. Good observation was obtained from the crest of the hill about 400 yards in front of the Btys. Many fleeting targets in and about DESTREMONT Farm and LE SARS were successfully engaged during the day. Towards evening there places were captured, and preparations were made for further advance early the following morning.	
H.Q. M.2.d.9.6.	26		Positions were taken up outside the AQUEDUCT ROAD, just W. of LE SARS. To support attack which had as their objective the capture of BEAULENCOURT and the crossing of the BAPAUME – PERONNE Road. Rather more opposition than was expected was experienced in the sunken road near LUISENHOF FARM and our line on the high ground W. of BEAULENCOURT, was not established until the following day.	
H.Q. M.17.f.41.	28		The Brigade took up positions of readiness near EAUCOURT L'ABBAYE and was placed under the orders of G.O.C. 6 x 9 Bde. which was in support of the 110th Inf. Bde. Batteries were not called upon to do any firing from these positions.	
H.Q. N.13.d.	31		To assist in attack on BEAULENCOURT in the evening and on the Sugar Factory early the following morning. Batteries were moved forward to positions from 1800 to 1500 yards N. of GUEUDECOURT near the GUEUDECOURT – LIGNY-THILLOY Road. The evening attack on BEAULENCOURT did not succeed	

9th x Bde R.F.A.

WAR DIARY
or
INTELLIGENCE SUMMARY. (3)

Army Form C. 2118.

August 1918

Place	Date	Hour	Summary of Events and Information	Remarks and references to Appendices
Field			Casualties.	Sheet 57 D
	2		136197 Gnr Roor C. wounded in action (Gas). C Bty	
	6		154087 - Madduck F. " " " " "	
	7		179068 - Jorton W. " " " " "	
	8		252724 - Ward B. Killed in action	
	14		731357 - Whittaker wounded in action Gas	
	"		71096 Bor Carter J. " " " "	
	"		45706 Gnr Burrow H " " " "	
	24		77088 Sgt Allen R.R. wounded in action D	
	"		146651 Bdr Yelden a. " " " " "	
	"		83972 - Morley J " " " " "	
	"		209178 Gnr Wroot J " " " " "	
	"		104319 Dr Harden a " " " B (remained at duty)	
	27		75865 Gnr King C. " " " " "	
			Honors and Awards.	
			NIL	

27.9.18.

Lt Col R.F.A.
Comdg. 9th Brigade R.F.A.

Army Form C. 2118.

WAR DIARY
or
INTELLIGENCE SUMMARY

(Erase heading not required.)

9th A Brigade R.F.A.

Sept 1918.

No. of 37

Instructions regarding War Diaries and Intelligence Summaries are contained in F.S. Regs., Part II. and the Staff Manual respectively. Title pages will be prepared in manuscript.

Place	Date	Hour	Summary of Events and Information	Remarks and references to Appendices
H.Q. LUISENHOF FARM	1/2		Batteries from position N. of BUEDECOURT supported a successful attack by the buffs Bar on the CLAY PIT O.13.a H.2 and LUBDA COPSE	Att. 57 C
	2/3		An attack by 110th Inf Bde. on BEAULENCOURT succeeded in taking the village. Batteries were moved to positions W. of BEAULENCOURT N.16.d. and 24.b. early on morning of 3rd. (At D.A. order.)	
H.Q. Sunken Rd N24.a.	3		Came under the tactical control of C.R.A. 17th Div. Owing to the rapid relieving of the enemy, batteries were out of range by midday. Brigade remained in these positions & Brains were tried from C.R.A. 17th Div. were received about 9am for the Bde. to come into positions of readiness about O.22 and 28. At 2.30 pm owing to the infantry situation being of a swift nature orders were received from 17th Div. to come into action in positions of observation in the neighbourhood of the position of readiness. Position were taken up in O.22.d. and O.28.a. from where attack by the 17th Div. infantry on trench system between YTRES and ETRICOURT were supported.	
H.Q. Gun Pits O.28.d.6.1.8.	4		During the night the position of A.185, who changed to ammunition supply, was taken at first. Location was impossible under cover. At the 2nd position, Railway cutting, fire was directed on specified tracks frequently during the day. At 5.30 and 8.30 pm barrages were fired to support our attack. In accordance with 17th Divl. Inst. ...	
H.Q. at CHATEAU SAILLY SAILLISEL	5		121 Bde R.F.A. the anchors took place between 8pm and midnight. Owing to the intense darkness and heavy rain batteries in some areas did not get into their new positions until daybreak on 6 inst. New positions taken up were E. of SAILLY SAILLISEL in U.15. 16.4.18.	
H.Q. Gun Pits V.14.A.	6		The enemy having retired from the Canal at MANANCOURT, the Bde. was ordered forward N. of the Canal, and Btys. took up positions in V.14.b. and d. and 20.a. The Bde. again came under orders of 21 DA, and supported the 62nd Inf. Bde. during the night of 6/7 d. EQUANCOURT, FINS and SOREL were occupied by our	
H.Q. V.14.B.5.	7		Battalions. A.185 moved forward to positions S. of SOREL LE GRAND. In bad of covering HEUDECOURT from then N. position. Attack were supported which resulted in the capture of REVILLON FARM	

Army Form C. 2118.

96 Brigade R.F.A.

WAR DIARY
or
INTELLIGENCE SUMMARY. (2.)

(Erase heading not required.)

Sept. 1918

Place	Date	Hour	Summary of Events and Information	Remarks and references to Appendices
	9		A.C. & D Batteries moved forward to positions S. of HEUDECOURT to support an attack on CHAPEL HILL. The attack failed.	Sheet 57c
	16		A Bty. of Bde. remained behind the O.R. Btys. of R. Bde. in position S. of SORBEL (GERMANS) moved forward in G.W.27.a with a view to an operation to take CHAPEL HILL and the ridge between there and PEIZIERES.	
	17		HQ in close liaison with 62nd Inf Bde for operations the following day.	
	18.		HQ moved about 9am to the BRICK YARD S. of HEUDECOURT (W.21.d) for the attack the Bns. an 72 Army Bdes R.F.A. came under command of 96th Bde R.F.A. The first phase of the attack in the early morning was most successful. Later in the day enemy moved forward on to at intervals during the day to positions S. of CHAPEL HILL W.24.a and with a view to supporting later advance of the 110 Inf Bde. B/B Battery taken over by D/96 from 62 Inf Bde. HQ first. Supplies of ammunition were sent forward to support troops & to the 110th Inf Bde. at W.18.d.1.3. During the night 19/20th 70/19 Inf Bde (33 Div) took over the line from 110th Inf Bde.	
	19			
	20		The 9th Bde R.F.A. came under tactical control of C.R.A. 33 Div. at 10am. Close liaison was maintained with 19th Inf Bde and later 100th Bde until the arrival of Artillery forces of 33 Div. on 23rd. During the day enemy artillery activity was great. An enemy enterprise attempted at dusk against line by 33 Div infantry—training in their application the capture of VILLERS GUISLAIN, MEATH POST, MEATH LANE, LIMERICK POST. None of these attacks were successful.	
	23		In accordance with the 33rd Div. orders, Bde HQ at W.18.d.1.2. moved back via ?? 15th Bde R.F.A. and the O.C. HQ of the 315 Army field R.F.A. at W.32.d. occupied the duties of liaison Officer, and 100th Bde. passed to O.P. 156 Bde at 7.30 am 23rd.	
	26		A single gun for sniping and all tank work was placed in position about X.25.b.d.d.	
	28		A general attack carried out in the early morning in conjuncture with British & French troops succeeded in clearing the enemy from VILLERS GUISLAIN and the high ground W. of the CANAL AH Bty. have never the left succeeded. To be still in touch with elements of the enemy. The Canal as ST QUENTIN. Elements of the enemy were believed to be still in trenches E. of PEIZIERE in X.19.d. B.O.C. followed closing the nights of 27th-28th and came into action in X.25.R.	

Army Form C. 2118.

WAR DIARY
INTELLIGENCE SUMMARY.

94th Bde R.F.A. (3)

Sept. 1918.

Instructions regarding War Diaries and Intelligence Summaries are contained in F. S. Regs., Part II. and the Staff Manual respectively. Title pages will be prepared in manuscript.

(Erase heading not required.)

Place	Date	Hour	Summary of Events and Information	Remarks and references to Appendices
	29		During the early hours of the morning the fact was established that the enemy had evacuated all ground N. of the Canal between HONNECOURT and VEND HUILLE. Our Bde fired single guns in harrassing fire just N. of Canal about x.17a.	
	30		Attempts made by 107 & 9 Bde to push patrols across the Canal in direction of LATERRIERE were frustrated by the enemy M.Guns on the E. bank of Canal. Sniping was carried out by B.Sgts from forward positions during the day with good results.	
			Honors and Awards	
			Gunner T. Badger and Dvr. A. Woodard A.15/94 awarded Military Medal. Gunner C. Rowe C/94 & Gnr F. Taylor B/94 awarded Croix de Guerre. Drivers E. Adcodon 15/94 awarded Military Medal. Brewer Cliff.	
			Casualties	
	4		Capt. L. Adams wounded in action A.B.L.	CBk
	4		70661 Dr. Smith H.a. " "	
	19		97803 Sgt. Vernon " "	
			36592 Gr. Brown " "	
			21547 Dr. Brown " "	
			287127 Gr. Smith " "	
			23304 " Luca "	
			31601 " Di Custer "	
			Major Cox alfully wounded in action (Gas) CBk	
			Capt. R. Ant. J. Luches " " "	
			Lt R. Pearce " " "	
			Lt J. Mellor " " "	
			Lt V. M. Coats " " "	
			114276 Gr. Right " " "	
			63933 Br. Mellor 28 " " "	
			101505 Sgt. Anderson " " "	
			732524 Gr. Drake 20/7 " " "	
			131424 Gnr. Senden C " " "	
			70706 " Kitchen L " " "	
				date	
			2 Lt. 900178 Gr. Gifkin F wounded in action (Gas)	CBk
			73562 " Thomas A " "	
			956037 " Lemme AP " "	
			140411 Dr. Edward A " "	
	16		17667 Sgt. Gandy R wounded in action	DBk
	19		125589 Gnr. Kearney J " "	"
	24		Major Cm Taylor wounded in action (Gas)	"

C. Anstuph
Lieut Col R.F.A.
Comdg. 94th Bde R.F.A.

H.Q.,
94th BRIGADE,
R.F.A.

No. ....
Date 2.10.18

CONFIDENTIAL.

WAR DIARY

OF

94th Brigade R.F.A.

FROM:- 1st October 1918.   TO:- 31st October 1918.

Army Form C. 2118.

WAR DIARY
or
INTELLIGENCE SUMMARY.

(Erase heading not required.)

94th Brigade R.F.A.

Instructions regarding War Diaries and Intelligence
Summaries are contained in F.S. Regs., Part II
and the Staff Manual respectively. Title pages
will be prepared in manuscript.

OCTOBER 1918.

Place	Date	Hour	Summary of Events and Information	Remarks and references to Appendices
H.Q. on PEZIERE VILLERS GUISLAN Rd.	1-5		Bde under 33rd D.A. was in posions in vicinity of QUAIL valley E. of PEZIERE. Enemy retired from HINDENBURG System on the front covered by the Bde during the of 4/5th OCT. Orders were recieved during the evening for the Bde to move across the CANAL DE ST QUENTIN, at BANTEUX in support of 110th INF. BDE. which was in Reserve.	
H.Q. M.22.b.7.1.	6		Bde again came under the command of C.R.A. 21 Div. Btys moved independently at dawn to a rendezvous at BANTOUZELLE. As a result of reconnaissance during the morning, positions were selected S. of Vaucelles Wood and occupied during the afternoon. The order at was only two Btys (B&C) to take up thier positions, but this was countermanded, with the result that A & D came into action c just before dark. D Bty was detailed to cut wire of the WALINCOURT—AUDIGNY Line on the Southern part of Divl. Front.	
H.Q. S.4.a.8.5.	7 8		D Bty continued wire cutting.
Barrages were fired 01.00, 05.15, and 08.00 hours. Bdy arrived section this attack which was cancelled at 08.00 hours. One section of 62nd Bde was ordered to front at BdM which also commenced forward to support. Close liaison was maintained with Battn. Commdrs. all day and much useful work was done. This was more especailly so in the case of the section from A Bty under the command of 2/Lt. CHAPMAN, D.S.O. which on one occaision turned captured 77m.m. guns on the enemy with great effect. At about 09.30 hours Btys were moved forward to positions in N.26.
A barrage was commenced at 18.00 hours in support of an attack on WALINCOURT but this was stopped at 18.25 hours as it was found that our Infantry had already occupied the village.	
H.Q. MONTECOUVEY FARM.	9		Orders were recieved overnight to the effect that the 21st D.A. would come under the control of C.R.A. 17th Div. at 05.00 hours. The Bde was placed at the disposal of 17th D.A. for an early morning attack on the high ground N.18.a. N of SELVIGNY. This attack was cancelled as it was found that the enemy had gone futher back during the night. The Bde was ordered at 08.00 hours tom reconnoitre positions in N.17, 23, or 29 and to occupies these as soon as GARE Wood was held by our troops. Orders recieved from 17th D.A. at 09.00 hours to move Byts to positions in above mentioned squares at once as CAULLERY was now in our hands.
When reconnoitring parties arrived on the high ground in N. 18.a. at about 10.30 hours it was seen that the enemy had gone much further back and Btys would consequently be out of effective range if they came into action in the positions which had been ordered.
Btys were therefore ordered to rendezvous N. of SELVIGNY, and a reconnoitring party under the Bde Commdr. went forward to high ground between CAULLERY AND MONTIGNY. As a result of this reconnaissance A Bty was brought into action E. of CAULLERY (O.9.a.8.2.), and the remaining Btys moved to positions of readiness on the N.W. edge of the village of CAULLERY. From their positions A Bty did some excellent sniping during the afternoon on the area between CAUDRY & LETRONQUOY Far	

WAR DIARY or INTELLIGENCE SUMMARY

Army Form C. 2118.

94th BRIGADE R.F.A.

OCTOBER 1918

Place	Date	Hour	Summary of Events and Information	Remarks and references to Appendices
	10		Bde formed part of main body and was instructed not to move without orders from I7 B.A.. At 11.00 hours the Bde was ordered to positions of readiness near Montigny. On arrival of reconnoitering parties there, further orders were issued by I7 D.A.,for Btys to come into action in T.22.Con the Southern outskirts of Inchy to fire a barrage at I7.00 hours around Neuvilly where resistance had been met. Roads were very much congested and it was only by going across country through a great deal of ploughed fields, that Btys were able to get into positions in time. No registrations were carried out but the 50th Inf Bde expressed their satisfaction at the Barrage. The attack was not successful. New troops of a Jaeger Regt were met who put a very strong resistance with the result that after the village on both flanks, our troops were forced to retire to the line of the river. NEUVILLY WAS REPORTED to be a veritable nest of M.G. Btys were shelled intermittently during the night by 8''Hows.,A Bty who were forced to withdraw temporarily from their positions, had one gun put out of action and some ammunition blown up.	
H.Q. INCHY.	11		Horses and mules were now very exhausted as a result of continous heavy work during the past seven weeks No further attempt was made during the day by the Infantry to take NEUVILLY.Btys regestered and did a little sniping during the morning and early afternoon. Visibility became very poor at 15.00 hours	
	12		Orders recieved at 02.15 hours for an attack to be carried out by 52nd Inf. Bde. in conjunction with 33rd Div. with the object of taking NEUVILLY. and high E. of it. Barrage opened at 05.00 hours and continued until 06.12 hours The area K.10. a, and K.4.c. was kept under to assist a further operation by 52nd Bde.	
	13-15		Only sniping and harassing fire . Visibility generally very poor. During the night 15/16 Oct, the village of INCHY and the surroundings, including Bty positions was heavily shelled with Mustard Gas. Considering the intesity of the bombardment the number of casualities in the Bde was very small Heavy rain from about dawn and a liberal use of Choride of Lime undoubtedly prevented the developements.	
	16		Gas Shell at last became available for 18 pdrs, 1100rounds of "B.B."were drawn by the Bde.	
	17		Shoots were carried out by Btys as follows:-00.05 to 00.30 hours Gas shoot on Sunken Road and Tramway in K.3.d. and K.9.b. Bursts of harassing fire of 5.minutes duration at 03.45 and 04.30. In conjunction with an operation carried out by 4th Army a Chinese Barrage was put down E. of NEUVILLY from 07.42 to 08.24 hours. The morning turned very foggy at about 07.00 hours and it was only with great difficulty that Btys were able to lay their guns.	
	18		Btys moved at intervals between dawn and 09.00 hours to positions in J.18.c. and J.24.b.behind the crest, about 3000,yards W. of NEUVILLY..	
	19		The day was spent in getting up large quantities of ammunition and in generally preparing for the attack timed for the following morning Concentrations of 5minutes were fired at 06.00, 10.25, 18.00, and 22.30 on points of probable resistance.	

Army Form C. 2118.

94th BRIGADE R.F.A.

Instructions regarding War Diaries and Intelligence Summaries are contained in F.S. Regs., Part II. and the Staff Manual respectively. Title pages will be prepared in manuscript. OCTOBER. 1918½

WAR DIARY or INTELLIGENCE SUMMARY.

(*Erase heading not required.*)

Place	Date	Hour	Summary of Events and Information	Remarks and references to Appendices
	20		Barrage opened at 02.00 hours and continued until 08.05 hours. The object of the attack, which was carried out in four stages, was to take AMERVAL and the high ground E. of NEUVILLY. About 09.00 hours fire was concentrated on the Left of the Divnl. front against a concentrated counter attack which was developing. This counter attack was stopped. Owing to bad visibility and the constant fluctuation of the line due to small local counter attacks, the situation was not clear until late in the evening, when it was found that the final objective had been taken throughout except for a pocket in AMERVAL. Orders were received about 16.30. for the Bde to cross the R. SERRE over night and to come into action at dawn on the rising ground N.E. of NEUVILLY.	
	21		Btys moved at about 04.00 hours in a downpour of rain. The bridge N. of NEUVILLY by which the Bde was ordered to cross the R. SERRE, led on to a ploughed field. Here Guns and Wagons even with 12 & 16 horse teams got stuck fast in the soft ground. In most cases wagons had to be unloaded and the ammunition sent to the gun positions by pack animals. Bde again came under orders of C.R.A. 21 Div. at 12.00 hours.	
H.Q. NEUVILLY	23		The Bde did not take part in the barrage which opened at 02.00 hours, but stood ready to go forward to positions from which it could support 62md Bde in the 3rd & 4th phases of the attack the objects of which were the capture of VENDEGIES & POIX du NORD. Btys rendezvoused in positions of readiness between AMERVAL & OVILLERS at 07.00 hours B&C Btys moved forward into action S. of OVILLERS at about 11.00 hours and were followed by A & D Btys just before dusk. For all operations after the initial phase of the attack on this day 95th, 78th, 79th Bdes R.F.A., the 34th Army F.A. Bde, 2 Sections of the 135th Bde R.G.A. (60 pdrs) and 6 Mobile T.M's were placed under the control of O/C 94th Bde R.F.A. (Lt.Col. BOYD,D.S.O.) LINCOLN Sections from A & E Btys were detailed to keep in close support of 1st & 2nd Battns respectively. Close touch was maintained by these sections with Battn. Commdrs all day, but opportunities for effective were few owing to poor visibility and nature of ground. H.Q. wrer established in OVILLERS during the evening.	
H.Q. OVILLERS	24		An attack at 04.00 hours on POIX du NORD by 62nd & 64 th Inf. Bdes was supported by fire from all Btys. This attack succeeded and A,B,D, Btys moved forward to positions E. of VENDEGIES, just in time to fire a barrage for an attack at 1600 hours to capture ground of tactical importance E. of POIX du NORD. C Bty which had become much reduced in personnel owing to evacuations due to influenza, did not move forward from its positions at OVILLERS.	
	26		Barrage fired at 01.00 in support of attack by 110th Inf. Bde. to establish posts on a line approximately from S.13.d.4.3. to X.11.b.3.0.	

Army Form C. 2118.

WAR DIARY
or
INTELLIGENCE SUMMARY.

94th BRIGADE R.F.A.

OCTOBER 1918.

Place	Date	Hour	Summary of Events and Information	Remarks and references to Appendices
H.Q. VENDEGIES.	26		At 13.00 hours orders were recieved for the Bde to withdraw to CLARY for 3 days rest. Btys moved independently during the afternoon and arrived at CLARY between 22.00hours and 01.00 hours 27th. Fairly good billets were obtained- Officers and N.C.O!s in houses, O.R.s in straw barns.	
	30		The Bde returned to the line, arriving between 2000hours. A.B.&D. Btys returned to the positions N.E. of VENDEGIES which they had vacated on 26th inst. C Bty took up a position in the same vicinity.	
	31		Harassing fire was carried out by all Btys at the rate of 300 rounds per 18pdr, and 200 rounds per How Bty per day.	
			HONORS and AWARDS. NIL.-	
			CASUALTIES.	
"A" Bty			173933 Bdr Audsley H. Wounded 'GAS' 19/10/18.	
"			77558 Dr. Rice G. Killed 22/10/18.	
"			179126 " Edwards S. Wounded 23/10/18.	
"			22404 Sgt. Underwood G. Killed 30/10/18.	
"			19885 " Ibertson E. Wounded "	
"			234955 Gnr Cann N.S. " "	
"			135475 " Hart W. " "	
"			35030 " Lee A.E. " "	
"			63587 Dr. Pickering T. " "	
"			203796 Gnr Triggle W. " "	
			No.34629 Cpl. Crownshaw E. Killed, 4/10/18. 'C' Bty.	
			" 92884 Gnr. Turner R. " " "	
			" 88779 Bdr. Barker R.W. " " "	
			731374 Gnr. Schofield S. Wounded " "	
			236676 " Woodburn A.E. " " "	
			219667 " Brown H.H. " " "	
			73562 " Thorpe S. 'Died' GAS' " "	
			2127173Gnr. Thomas G.A. Wounded 1/10/18. 'D' Bty.	
			876169 Cpl Moore T. " 8/10/18. "	
			715215 Gnr. Walker D. " 10/10"18 "	
			558874 " Evans C. " 25/10/18 "	
			154986 " Gray D. " 24/10/18 "	
			72300 Sgt. Curley " 17/10/18. "	
			241549 Gnr. Blaylock G. " " (GAS)	
"B" Bty			122222 Cpl. Overton C. Wounded 24/10/18.	
"			137393 Gnr Readyough " "	
"			87602 " Watts W.J. " "	
"			224859 " Cooper R.S. " "	
" 2 "			237932 " Smee P. Wounded 'GAS' 16/10/18.	
"			955352 Cpl. Beckley " "	
"			67686 Bdr. Gramham " "	
"			875326 Gnr Kelly R " v 17/10/18.	
"			655773 " Browning " "	
"			760751 Sgt. Balsom E. " 19/10/18½	
"			34783 Dr. Nichols E. " 21/10/18.	
			846165 Bdr. Talbot W. Wounded 'GAS' 22/10/18.	
			91526 Gnr. Savage J. " "	
			223417 " Todd G.H. " "	
			6/11/18. COMMDG. 94th BRIGADE R/F/A. MAJOR RFA.	

C O N F I D E N T I A L.

WAR DIARY

OF

94th Brigade R.F.A.

FROM 1st November 1918. TO 30th November 1918.

Army Form C. 2118.

WAR DIARY
of
INTELLIGENCE SUMMARY.

94th Brigade. R.F.A.

Instructions regarding War Diaries and Intelligence Summaries are contained in F.S. Regs., Part II. and the Staff Manual respectively. Title pages will be prepared in manuscript.

NOVR. 1918.

(*Erase heading not required.*)

Place	Date	Hour	Summary of Events and Information	Remarks and references to Appendices
H.Q. VENDEGIES.	1-3		Brigade was in action near VENDEGIES-AU-BOIS. Brigade moved forward to positions S.E. of POIX-DU-NORD during the afternoon and came under the tactical control of C.R.A. 17th Div.	
H.Q. POIX-DU-NORD.	4-7		Barrage fired from 15-30 hours till about 11-00 hours in support of attack on FORET-de-MORMAL. Owing to a very severe epidemic of influenza which had broken out in all Batteries rendering them immobile, orders were recieved for the Bde to remain at POIX-DU-NORD. Batteries moved into the village, and wagon-lines joined Batteries on the 5th.	
H.Q. LA GRAND CARRIERE	8		Orders were recieved overnight that owing to the difficulty of supplies, the Brigade would move forward to LOCQUIGNOL, or further if the situation permitted. Batteries marched at 10-00 hours to the neighboorhood of BERLAIMONT. Accomodation for one Battery only was available at BERLAIMONT, and the Brigade, less "A" Battery, moved to billets at LA GRAND CARRIERE.	
	9-14		H.Q.,"B,C,D, Btys remained at LA GRAND CARRIERE. "A" Battery at BERLAIMONT.	
	15		Orders had been recieved the previous day for the Brigade to move to billets at NEUVILLY. Owing to the congestion of traffic on the roads, the march was carried out by night, commencing at 23-15 hours.	
H.Q. NEUVILLY.	16		The Brigade arrived at NEUVILLY at 05-00 hours, and occupied billets.	
	17-30		Batteries carried out schemes of training. "A" and "D" Batteries were inspected by the C.R.A. on 25th NOVR., and "B" and "C" Batteries on 26th NOVR.	

HONOURS & AWARDS.

| | 28 | | Lieut-Colonel H.A. BOYD, D.S.O., Awarded " Chevalier du Legion d' Honneur." | |

CASUALTIES.

No 34291 Bomdr. Eyres J.W. Wounded in Action, 3/11/18. "B" Battery.
66720 Dvr. Willets R. " "(GAS) 3/11/18 "B" "

10/12/18.

[signature]
Major, R.F.A.
Commanding 94th Brigade R.F.A.

CONFIDENTIAL.

WAR DIARY

OF

94th Brigade R.F.A.

FROM:- December 1st.   TO:- December 31st 1918.

94th Brigade R.F.A. Army Form C. 2118.

Instructions regarding War Diaries and Intelligence
Summaries are contained in F.S. Regs., Part II.
and the Staff Manual respectively. Title pages
will be prepared in manuscript.

WAR DIARY
or
INTELLIGENCE-SUMMARY.
(Erase heading not required.)

DECEMBER 1918.

Place	Date	Hour	Summary of Events and Information	Remarks and references to Appendices
NEUVILLY	1-12.		Brigade in Billets. Batteries continued with schemes of training. On 4th inst H.M. The King visited NEUVILLY and inspected Brigade.	
	13.		Brigade moved to WALINCOURT at 08.00 hours, via TROISVILLES, CLARY, and SELVIGNY. Brigade reached WALINCOURT at about 14.30 hours and occupied billets.	
	14.		Brigade moved to BRUSLE at 07.30 hours, via VILLERS-OUTREAUX, VEDHUILE, ROISEL, and TINCOURT. Brigade reached BRUSLE at 16.00 hours and occupied huts and bivouacs.	
	15.		Brigade moved to PROYART at 08.00 hours, via BRIE, FOUCANCOURT. Reached PROYART about 15.00 hours, and occupied billets and bivouacs.	
	16.		Brigade moved to BLANGY at 07.30 hours, via VILLERS-BRETTONNEUX. Reached BLANGY at 14.00 hours and occupied huts.	
	17.		Brigade moved to LA CHAUSSEE at 07.30 hours, avoiding AMIENS by the South. Reached LA CHAUSSEE at 13.00 hours.	
	18-31		Brigade in Billets at LA CHAUSSEE. Accomodation for men and horses was poor, necessitating the building of huts for the men, while horse lines had to be put on the roads, as no other land ground could be found. Time was mostly spent in improving Billets and recreation.	

HONOURS & AWARDS.

Lieut-Colonel H.A. BOYD, D.S.O., Awarded C.M.G., H.Q.

2/Lieut. G.P. CHAPMAN, D.S.O., Awarded M.C., "A" Battery.

4.1.19.

Lieut-Col. R.F.A.
Commanding 94th Brigade R.F.A.

WAR DIARY
or
INTELLIGENCE SUMMARY.

(Erase heading not required.)

94th Brigade R.F.A.   Army Form C. 2118.

January, 1919.

Place	Date	Hour	Summary of Events and Information	Remarks and references to Appendices
LA CHAUSSÉE	1-31		Brigade still in Billets and Huts. Many Huts have been erected, and the men are much more comfortable now. Recreational training carried during the whole month, also education facilities are much better.	Sheet 62E 1/40,000.
			The Brigade sent 120 horses to AMIENS for sale on the 16th inst.	
	20.2.1919.			

[signature]
Lieut-Colonel R.F.A.
Commanding 94th Brigade R.F.A.

C O N F I D E N T I A L

WAR DIARY

OF

94th Brigade R. F. A.

FROM:- 1st February 1919. TO:- 28th February 1919.

Army Form C 2118 (MS)

94th BRIGADE R.F.A.

WAR DIARY

FEBRUARY 1919.

Place.	Date.	Hour.	Summary of events and information.	Remarks and references to Appendices.
LA CHAUSSEE	1-31		Brigade still in billets and huts. Nothing of special interest has occured during the month.	
			Brigade Sports were held on the 25th which proved to be fairly successful, also recreational training was carried out through the whole month.	
			The Brigade was reduced to Cadre "B" by about the 15th inst.	
			Animals were sold at AMIENS, POIX and HORNOY.	

13.3.1919

Major, R.F.A.
Commanding 94th Brigade R.F.A.

Army Form. C 2118 (M.S.)

WAR ------------ DIARY6

MARCH---------1919.

94th BRIGADE R.F.A.

Place	Date.	Hour.	Summary events and information.	Remarks and references to appendices.
LA CHAUSSEE	1-31.		Brigade still in billets and huts. Nothing of special interest has occured during the month.	
			All Guns and vehicles taken down to Cadre Park LONGPRE, with exceptionef of Water-carts. Mobilization Stores was also taken to Cadre Park and arranged for inspection by Ordnance.	
			The Brigade was reduced to Cadre "A" about the 22nd., all remaining horses were sold at sales administered by A.D.V.S. V Cprps.	
			Lieut. R.S. KING, R.F.A. took up the duties of Sub-Area Commandant LONG, also an Officer was detailed to be in charge of Brigade Stores at the Cadre Park LONGPRE.	
			Recreational Training is still being carried out, but on rather a small scale.	

1.4.1919

2/Lieut, R.F.A.

For Officer Commanding 94th Brigade R.F.A.

WAR DIARY

FEBRUARY 1919

Army Form C.2118 (MS)

94 Bde RFA VSl 44

WAR DIARY.
for APRIL, 1919.

94th BRIGADE R.F.A.   Summary of Events and Information.

Place	Date	Hour	
LA CHAUSSEE.	1st-4th.		Brigade fully reduced to Cadre "A". All vehicles with the exception of Water Carts were removed to Cadre Park LONGPRE, also all Mobilization Stores.
	4th-30th.		Brigade moved to LONG on the morning of the 4th and occupied billets the same night. Recreational Training carried out on a very small scale, but the men appear to be fairly comfortable.
			Inspection of Mobilization Stores at the Cadre Park was carried out by Ordnance Officer on the 25th.
			Nothing more of special interest has occured during the month.

2.5.1919

Major, R.F.A.
Commanding 94th Brigade R.F.A.

www.ingramcontent.com/pod-product-compliance
Lightning Source LLC
Chambersburg PA
CBHW081530160426
43191CB00011B/1725